# BARTY

## Much More Than Tennis

Ron Reed and Chris McLeod

WP

Published by:
Wilkinson Publishing Pty Ltd
ACN 006 042 173
PO Box 24135, Melbourne, VIC 3001, Australia
Ph: +61 3 9654 5446
enquiries@wilkinsonpublishing.com.au



WilkinsonPublishing
wilkinsonpublishinghouse
WPBooks



NATIONAL LIBRARY OF AUSTRALIA
A catalogue record for this book is available from the National Library of Australia

Title: Barty: Much More Than Tennis
ISBN(s): 9781925927801: Printed — Paperback

Front cover: 9 February 2021: Melbourne, Australia. Ash Barty of Australia celebrates winning her first round match against Danka Kovinic of Montenegro at the 2021 Australian Open at Melbourne Park.
(Photo by Michael Klein / Newspix.)

Transcripts from by ASAP Sports.
Statistics from WTA Press Center.

Design: Michael Bannenberg
Printed and bound in Australia by Griffin Press

# CONTENTS

## LINDA PEARCE



## CHRIS McLEOD

# INTRODUCTION

Sports fans everywhere love a feel-good story, Australians are certainly no exception. If it involves fresh young talent taking on the world and winning against the odds, so much the better. That's why the coming of age of a brilliant new star in one of the nation's favourite sports, tennis, has been one of the most captivating highlights of the second decade of the 21st century — not just in a sporting context but in public life too.

Ashleigh Barty's reign as the world's best female player began just before the Coronavirus pandemic catastrophically disrupted life and was still firmly in place two years later as her ever-smiling, can-do, will-do attitude provided an inspirational focal point for Australians and a nation wondering whether life would ever be the same again.

In that time, she won two of the world's four biggest tournaments — the 2019 French Open and the 2021 Wimbledon — and held the No. 1 ranking for more than 80 weeks — and counting. It made her Australia's pre-eminent international sporting identity in the eyes of many.

A knockabout kid from Queensland whose rare gift for the game, engaging personality, innate modesty and relentless determination to be the best she could be was just about the perfect package, a throwback to the golden age of Australian tennis.

In a year of unrelenting achievement in 2019 she not only established herself as the leading female player but one of the most popular, certainly in her own country where she captured the imagination of aficionados of all things sporting and the community in general.

She was only 23 at that stage, her remarkable journey still well short of its ultimate destination with at least another decade in which to enhance her status as a legend in the making.

Bringing her childhood dream to life by winning Wimbledon — the ultimate achievement for almost any tennis player — was another huge step in that process, and she was still only 25, with the sky still the limit.

Who knows where it will end?

Even by the time she ascended to greatness on the famous clay courts of Paris, her story had so many elements to it that it was already time to assemble them in the form of a book, the first but certainly not the last to be written about her.

That book, *Barty: Power and Glory*, now demands an update because so much of importance has happened since, the title now changing to *Barty: Much More Than Tennis*.

This rewarding task has been led by one of Australia's best and most experienced sportswriters, Ron Reed, with expert assistance from another accomplished senior journalist, Chris McLeod, and an insightful contribution from veteran tennis writer Linda Pearce.

Reed is a veteran of more than half a century in newspapers, almost all of it at the Herald and Weekly Times in Melbourne where he was Editor of the now defunct *Sporting Globe*, twice

Sports Editor of the afternoon daily *The Herald* and Chief Sportswriter and Contributing Editor of the *Herald Sun*, Australia's biggest-selling newspaper.

He has reported on international sport from every continent and more than 30 countries, including nearly 20 Olympic and Commonwealth Games, cricket tours to almost everywhere the game is played at Test level, several editions of the Tour de France and Italian Giro bike races, world title fights, major tennis and golf championships, the America's Cup yachting and world championships in athletics, road and track cycling, triathlon, rowing, hockey, squash and weightlifting, as well as horse racing and all the football codes.

He has won many writing awards, including Sportswriter of the Year and a Lifetime Achievement Award from the Australian Sports Commission.

He has written six other books, including an acclaimed biography of another tennis champion, Frank Sedgman, as well as *War Games*, a well-received personal account of events and people who featured in his own journeys through domestic and international sport.

He continues to write on contemporary sport for his own website *sportshounds.com.au* and for *footyalmanc.com.au*.

McLeod is a former editorial and management executive with *The Herald* and the *Herald Sun*. He has a deep interest in sport, transport and history and is the author of *World's Best Golf Courses* and *World's Best Trains* bookazines. He is currently the author and researcher for floggerblogger.com.

Pearce has long been regarded as one of Australia's leading tennis journalists, having covered more than 50 Grand Slam tournaments and four Davis Cup finals and been named Australian tennis writer of the year twice as well as winning the ATP Ron Bookman Award for media excellence in the sport. She first interviewed Barty a decade ago and has followed her career closely, both at home and abroad.

1

# MUCH MORE THAN TENNIS

Of all the many uplifting sports stories that have captured the imagination of Australia as a nation — and they are legion, across many diverse disciplines, performed by men and women of all ages and backgrounds, and even by animals — few have been greeted with such spontaneous and unanimous acclaim as tennis champion Ashleigh Barty's Wimbledon triumph on 10 July 2021.

It has meant that "the Barty Party" — a cheerful term coined when she first asserted herself as the dominant female figure in international women's tennis two years earlier — no longer adequately conveys what her "brand" means in the eyes of the people she so proudly represents, or how valuable it has become in every sense.

There are many reasons for that. It is about much more than tennis. Indeed, she is well on the way to transcending sport itself.

Her unfolding, unfinished narrative has come to resonate with unusually intense overtones of national pride and inspiration, community morale, cultural issues ancient and modern, the importance of family and friends, the regard for humility and grace over rampant ambition and avarice, the escalating battle for gender equality, the banishment of the scourge of the ugly parent syndrome, and perspectives on fame and fortune.

Lessons in life, in other words.

If that seems a lot to lay at the doorstep of a laid-back kid from Queensland with no tickets on herself — and it is — then it is an accurate measure of how extraordinary her own life is turning out to be given that she is still only 25, perhaps less than halfway along her professional path, with the sky the limit to how far she might yet have to go.

If an explanation is required for how and why she has travelled so far, so quickly, so successfully and with such admiration and respect, almost to the point of public adoration, perhaps it is captured by the mantra which she has verbalised many times, and repeated again to the world's media in the immediate, euphoric aftermath of the biggest triumph of her life.

At her post-match press conference at Wimbledon, she said that it was more important to be a good human being than a good tennis player, and that being true to her values — instilled in her by her parents, Josie and Jim — were her priorities each and every day.

It sounds almost too good to be true, frankly. Nobody is perfect, we all know that. When writing a book about anybody, no matter how lionised and accomplished, it is usually incumbent on the author to avoid reducing it to mere hagiography, an obligation not always accepted or successfully executed. But for it to be truly warts and all, there have to be some warts to identify.

Those closest to Barty may or may not be able to point out a few, but the journalists who have laid waste to vast quantities of newsprint and filled countless hours of air-time have come up empty-handed in that respect, and the reality would certainly be that it wouldn't have been because none of them ever attempted it.

The media love nothing more than a good news story but, equally, there is no reluctance — and often a definite appetite — to shine a light on the dark side, if one can be found. Suffice to say, it has yet to happen in this case and there is no good reason to suspect that it ever will.

Just how immense was her triumph on the manicured lawns of London SW19, the repository of more tennis history than any other place on the planet? And why?

Cathy Freeman's immortal 400m golden lap of the Sydney Olympic Stadium in 2000 is unlikely ever to be usurped as the most emotional and memorable Australian sporting moment of the 21st century, and possibly the previous one too, but Barty has come as close as anyone has to providing an authentic rival to it.

For maybe a month she was perhaps the only one in the eyes of many — although a third candidate quickly arrived when swimmer Ariarne Titmus ignited the national mood when she twice defeated American superstar Katie Ledecky — widely-regarded as the best female swimmer in history — as the Tokyo Olympics exploded into action. There were many new Australian heroes created at those Games but Titmus set the pace and the tone and will arguably be remembered best.

For Freeman and Barty, perhaps "rival" is not the appropriate word for it; their stories are companion pieces.

No-one would be happier about that than Freeman herself for the pair are, in a very real sense, sisters, together with another iconic figure from the same sport as Barty, Evonne Goolagong Cawley.

In search of reasons why Barty's win matters so much to the Australian psyche — and there are a multitude of them — this is a very good place to start.

Together, the three of them are linked by cultural, social and political history stretching back to the dawn of time and yet as modern as tomorrow.

That's because they are all Indigenous, as well as being female — in an age of enlightenment and unprecedented respect for women's sport — and all intelligent, articulate, modest, humble and proud role models for successive generations of not just people with whom they share an ancient heritage, but Australians of every ilk.

It would be a challenge to identify any group of three Australians with a common denominator — in any walk of life — who have enjoyed such unqualified collective popularity.

For Barty, that had already been the case for at least two years, since she dominated the circuit in 2019, rising to No. 1 in the world rankings and winning one of the four major tournaments that make up the Grand Slam, the French Open, for the first time, as well as the year-end championship and two other significant events.

It wasn't just what she won — far from it — but the way she went about it, marrying a towering and maturing talent with an ever-smiling, down-to-earth, laid-back personality that defied even opponents to dislike her, no matter how fiercely they might have been attempting to disrupt her mental and physical command of the rectangular battlefields that form the stage for a sport that does theatre as well as any when the cast are on their game.

For Barty, that was highly unlikely to ever change and never has, certainly not when the ultimate moment of truth arrived.

When she sealed the 6-3 6-7 (4-7) 6-3 victory over Czech Karolina Pliskova at 1.04 on a Sunday morning back in Australia — with bulging TV ratings confirming that seemingly everyone in the country had tuned in, kids long past their bedtime no exception — the applause was not only unrelenting for days on end, but totally without any suggestion of ho-hum, let alone negativity or carping about this or that.

Such total positivity is very rare in sport or anywhere else.

Why was that so? Answer: because there were so many authentic feel-good elements to it.

Not the least was the manner in which the combatants — both of them — went about it, no grunting, no arguments with linesmen or the umpire, no smashed racquets, no mumbled cursing, just a pure exhibition of tennis the way it is meant to be played.

That it went the full three sets with the momentum swinging from side to side, always an essential ingredient of truly great sport, added enormously to the spectacle, not so much a bonus as a guarantee that the experience had been all that it could and should be.

But on another level, the Goolagong-Cawley connection added a special, almost exquisite layer of meaning, which you didn't have to be Australian to absorb. Any sports lover would find it irresistible.

It was 50 years — a golden anniversary in any context — since Evonne realised exactly the same childhood dream, winning Wimbledon for the first time, but not the last. She went on to take the title again nine years later, as well as five other major tournaments while becoming the first Australian to hold the No. 1 ranking in 1975, a computerised statistic that did not officially exist when the legendary Margaret Court, winner of three Wimbledons and 24 majors in all, was in her imperious prime in the immediate previous era.

Now 70, a milestone she reached in the same month as Barty's win, Cawley has always been one of the most-loved figures in Australian life, sporting or otherwise, which speaks to her character — but also to the natural class and style with which she played the game. It's what often elevates good players in any sport to another level of magnetism.

She has been a friend, mentor and spiritual inspiration for Barty throughout the Queenslander's career, especially when it was interrupted briefly when the young star in the making, in need of mental refreshment, took time out to play cricket while she refocused on the main game.

Wimbledon was desperate to have Cawley on hand for the occasion, to at least celebrate the milestone anniversary whether or not Barty was able to emulate her, but their offer of first-class travel and accommodation and all the trimmings had to be declined because her husband Roger was ill and unable to accompany her.

Barty honoured her by wearing, in every match, a scalloped, flowery dress modelled on the one Cawley graced during her first year of glory, and although the tribute wasn't intended to be a good-luck symbol as such, that's what it turned out to be.

Barty, whose paternal links are to the Ngagaru people, and Cawley, who is a Wiradjuri woman, have known each other since Barty was 15, and they form a mutual admiration society.

"Evonne is a very special person in my life," Barty has often said. "I hope I made her proud," she added when she was presented with the trophy on centre court.

"She made me proud the first time I saw her," Cawley responded. "I think she has been iconic in paving the way for young Indigenous youth to believe in their dreams and to chase their dreams. She's done exactly that for me as well."

Freeman enthusiastically seconded the sentiment. "Massive pride in our girl. So proud of you," she tweeted.

It also was lost on no-one, of any background, that the

second week of Wimbledon was National Aborigines and Islanders Day Observance Committee (NAIDOC) week in Australia, in which culture and achievements of the first people are celebrated.

The Cawley anniversary wasn't the only almost eerie milestone that came into play. Barty had won the Wimbledon junior title exactly a decade earlier, so there was a certain sense that this outcome was written in the stars. She felt it too, even if she would never have said so beforehand. "The stars aligned for me," she said afterwards.

But fate can be a fickle friend.

Certainly there was nothing straightforward or easily predictable about the path forward after the heady, honour-heavy march through the breakout year of 2019.

The next year had barely begun when the COVID-19 pandemic turned the world upside down with tragic and far-reaching consequences for just about every country and institution, international sport definitely no exception.

For the first time since the Second World War, Wimbledon was unable to take place. The other Grand Slam events proceeded under great difficulty but for Barty it was almost a totally lost year, playing just four tournaments in Australia before deciding that defending her French crown was untenable and that she would stay home.

At least it gave her the chance to pursue two of her other diverse sporting loves, cheering on her beloved Richmond Tigers from the grandstand — beer in one hand, fist-pumping with the other — as they won the Australian Football League premiership for the third time in four years, upon which she was delighted to be offered the opportunity of presenting the Cup to her long-time mate, team captain Trent Cotchin.

If she had time to play footy herself, as women are now doing with increasing professionalism in Australia, she almost certainly would, just to prove there is no sport she cannot master to an impressive degree.

During the enforced lay-off the one-time professional cricketer and handy junior netballer also reduced her golf handicap from 10 to four while winning her local Brookwater Golf Club championship with a decisive seven-and-five win in the matchplay final, watched approvingly by her boyfriend Garry Kissick, a trainee professional.

The pandemic was still very much "a thing" as 2021 dawned, Barty determined to return to something approaching business as usual. Statistically and emotionally, the home-town heroine — still ranked No. 1 — was installed as a warm favourite for the Australian Open but made it only as far as the quarter-finals, losing in three sets to Czech Karolina Muchova.

But at least she was up and running again, as was the tennis circuit by and large.

Dog-eared passport in hand again, it was like she had never been away as she won important tournaments in Miami and Stuttgart and made a final in Madrid in preparation for Paris and

London. She looked to be in exceptionally fine fettle.

But in Rome in May, she retired while leading a quarter-final against precocious American Coco Gauff, citing an arm injury while also playing with strapping on her left thigh.

For her fans and support team, this was an unmistakeable alarm bell, but she claimed to be unfazed, saying the arm problem dated back 10 years and had always been manageable.

The thigh and hip seemed to present a bigger question mark, but it didn't prevent her lining up at Roland Garros, back at the scene of her greatest triumph so far.

However, after accounting for American Bernarda Pera in three sets in the first round, the hip was giving her so much grief that she then retired hurt at 6-1 2-2 against Poland's Magda Linette, to her enormous and obvious disappointment.

The alarm bells grew louder.

She admitted that it had been a miracle to get on the court at all and that she had shed "my fair share of tears this week". Typically, she remained upbeat. "Everything happens for a reason," she said.

"There will be a silver lining in this eventually. Once I find out what that is, it'll make me feel a little bit better, but it will be there, I'm sure."

By no means for the first or last time, her sense of perspective proved to be perfectly honed.

Her support team, headed by veteran coach Craig Tyzzer, physical performance coach Matt Hayes, physiotherapist Melanie

Omizzolo and mental conditioning mentor Ben Crowe, were considerably less optimistic.

They doubted the three-week recovery period would be enough to get her on deck at Wimbledon, and even if it somehow was, her prospects wouldn't be helped by the usual grass-court lead-up events being out of the question. But they decided not to spell that out for her and to see what happened.

So Barty either didn't know how bad the injury was — or didn't want to know. Obviously, it was going to be touch and go. So she just gritted her teeth and went for it — all the way to Centre Court on day two of The Championships, as the great tournament is officially known, just as the golf version is simply The Open, the emphasis on the word "the" as if all other championships and Opens are inherently inferior. It's a very British affectation, but probably true enough.

There, seemingly fully recovered, she started her campaign, with a valuable head start, namely the absence of world No. 2 Naomi Osaka, still uncertain about her precarious mental health, and the defending champion, from 2019, Romania's Simona Halep, because of a calf injury. The always formidable Serena Williams quickly followed, injuring herself in her first match.

Click. Click. You could hear the pieces already starting to fall into place.

Barty began against Spain's Carla Suarez Navarro, a cancer survivor nearing the end of a substantial career, and won in three sets, 6-1 6-7 (1-7) 6-1 with extra applause for publicly acknowledging her opponent's resilience and fighting spirit, saying it was a privilege to share a court with her.

One down, six to go — whoever they might be.

And so it proceeded.

Next came Russian Anna Blinkova, three years her junior and ranked 89, despatched rapidly and comfortably 6-4-6-3 despite an unusually high number of unforced errors.

Czech Katerina Siniakova, 25, ranked 64 and fresh from a grass-court final at Strasbourg a week earlier, made little impression, going down 6-3 7-5 in the third round.

Another Czech Barbora Krejicikova, the 14th seed who had just succeeded Barty as the French champion, opened up an early 2-4 lead but was overcome 7-5 6-3 as the tournament entered the crucial second week, where the big boys and girls live.

The quarter-final had an extra emotional edge to it because it was against another Australian, albeit one imported from Croatia mid-career in Aila Tomlianovic, 28, her new country's second-ranked player. Barty showed her no mercy, winning 6-1 6-3 and giving thanks for simply being able to do what she enjoys most, given the troubled state of the world around her.

The semi-final threw up the most threatening challenge so far, German Angelique Kerber, ranked 28, seeded 25, winner of three Grand Slam tournaments including Wimbledon in 2018. In a contest she described as "the best level I've played in some time" Barty prevailed 6-3 6-7 (4-7) 6-3 and said it had been fun.

These relaxed comments — "I'm just enjoying myself, having

fun" — resonated powerfully because they were such a very Barty-esque thing to say, given the stakes that were now in play.

Her lifetime dream was now sharply in focus — within tantalising, touching distance.

For many athletes in all sports, this would now be do or die. For Barty tennis has never been a matter of life or death. However, that is certainly not to suggest that she approaches it with anything less than everything she has to give so it would have been a massive mistake to suggest that her unflappable attitude and outlook meant that she was anything but switched

**"I'm just enjoying myself, having fun"**

on to the max, utterly determined to do justice to herself and everyone round her.

In one country, and one country only, the Czech Republic, sports fans would have been excused if they were starting to wish the ubiquitous Australian would just go away because having despatched two of their best hopes, she was now the only obstacle to a third one, Karolina Pliskova, the other finalist.

Like Barty, Pliskova, the eighth seed, was in the Wimbledon decider for the first time so it loomed as a battle of not just talent, but composure, nerve and poise.

That was confirmed emphatically when Barty reeled off the first 14 points, racing to a 4-0 lead, while the much taller Pliskova, looking slightly haunted by the pressure, irritated perhaps, froze.

Barty took the set comfortably 6-3 and by early in the second stanza the result looked inevitable. It wasn't. Barty wavered, delivering a rare double fault as she served for it at 6-5. Pliskova rallied, forcing it into a tie-break, which she took 7-6 (7-4), and with it, priceless momentum.

It was all square and sport's eternal truth had come into play — it ain't over until it's over.

That said, Barty looked to be the better, more confident player and to have more in reserve and it would still have been a shock to most observers if she had not prevailed. She did, 6-3 — and within what seemed like the blink of an eye, but was probably about 20 minutes, a formal, no-frills version of her name — Miss A. Barty — had been stencilled onto the green honour board, officially putting her into the most elite company the sport has to offer.

While that was happening, she was looking for an appropriate way to mark the moment and chose one that had a famous precedent.

The author was fortunate enough to be on hand in 1987 — a decade before Barty was born — to watch Melbourne's Pat Cash clamber like an excited mountain goat into the grandstand to embrace his coach after defeating Ivan Lendl.

It was a celebration the staid old All-England Lawn Tennis and Croquet Club, founded in 1868, had never seen before.

A likeable larrikin with a few rough edges, that unexpected

encore saw Cash dubbed the Wild Colonial Boy by the English media, not disapprovingly but as a happy nod to his Australianess.

When Barty did the same thing, albeit a tad more elegantly, she wasn't called any such names but it was recognised as just one more confirmation that there is nobody who comes across as Australian more authentically, more obviously, than she does. She could never be mistaken for an American, a Briton or a South African.

At home, people still didn't go to bed when the last point was played, on a high and preferring to share the euphoria with her as best they could from the other side of the world.

It was that sort of occasion, a national celebration — wherever you were.

The cameras showed her being feted by real royalty, Prince William and his wife Kate, and tennis royalty, Billie Jean-King and Martina Navratilova, celebrated champions from a much earlier era.

The Duchess of Cambridge had already been on court to present her with the trophy, a sterling silver salver known as the Venus Rosewater Dish which dates back to 1886 and features the mythological figure of Temperance as well as other gods.

The future king observed that she had not seemed very nervous, a notion she was quick to politely correct. "Well, you hid it very well," he said.

It wasn't until she moved on to her team, leaning into her

boyfriend's embrace, still with the cameras focused intently on her every move and utterance, that the tears could not be held back any longer.

These were all images that will resonate in posterity just as powerfully as the expertly-tailored groundstrokes and pulsating serves, the hustle, the grit, the persistence, that had got her there.

There were other priorities, most notably to get on the phone to her family back in Ipswich, who had not been able to be there in person because of the pandemic travel restrictions.

There has been no more constantly recurring — or more sincere — theme than Barty's gratitude towards her team, which she never fails to refer to as "we" — never "me".

She never forgets, ignores or downplays.

Her childhood coach Jim Joyce, to whom she has always remained close, and who had spent the day at the Rockhampton races before the biggest winner of his life saluted many thousands of kilometres away, received a simple text: "We've done it, Jimbo!"

In Melbourne, Tennis Australia chief executive Craig Tiley was ordering in crates of champagne for a Monday lunchtime party at the home of the Australian Open, needing no reminder what a massive fillip this was for the sport, especially among kids but also sponsors, influencers and fans. Asked on radio if Barty was now the nation's pre-eminent sports star, he said of course she was — and no-one attempted to argue.

But it's value was broader than that. Tennis wasn't the only context. Most of the country, especially the two biggest cities, Sydney and Melbourne, were in desperate need of a morale sugar-hit as they continued to struggle with the social and economic ravages of the pandemic, with millions of people losing livelihoods, their health and in too many cases, their lives. They were either locked down — under virtual house arrest — or about to be, for what seemed the umpteenth time.

The national mood needed a circuit-breaker.

Suddenly, in the letters pages in newspapers, on talkback radio and in social media, the daily outpouring of scorn, criticism, confusion and anger towards the various Governments and other authorities dealing with the drawn-out crisis was leavened by, if not almost entirely replaced, temporarily, with what amounted to a communal love letter to the central figure in this very welcome good news story.

It didn't make the virus disappear, alas, but for a couple of days, at least, it all seemed just that little bit less threatening.

There were many aspects to the tsunami of positivity. The Indigenous angle was high on the list, if not the top of it, of course, but so was gender, and for not dissimilar reasons.

After far too many years of struggling for opportunity and recognition, battling discrimination and disrespect, distaff sport has become a huge presence in the last few years and where once the media was reluctant or not engaged enough to fully acknowledge advancements and achievements, now there is seldom any holding back. If that means it sometimes gets a tad out of proportion in the other direction — and it undoubtedly does —

then that is not worth quibbling about, and nobody does.

Tennis is one sport where it's never been an issue anyway. And it's certainly not now. Barty is not the only racquet-wielder who has been provided with exposure and applause commensurate with her deeds, she — and the media-savvy management team guiding her — have just been better than most at maximising it in a way that is appealing, interesting and difficult to find fault with.

It is hard to say whether Osaka, who pulled out of the French Open early and then skipped Wimbledon because she found her media commitments too hard to handle, would be envious of her main rival's consummate charm and deft, easy performance in this important but sometimes tricky space, but it is certainly a stark contrast in not a good way.

So naturally Barty dominated the front pages of the Sunday papers within hours of her big moment. But not exclusively. Melbourne's Herald Sun, for instance, headlined its late edition LEGENDS — plural, not singular — and included a second photo.

That was because in their own backyard a few hours earlier, at Caulfield racecourse, another female superstar, jockey Jamie Kah, had completed the unprecedented feat of riding 100 winners at metropolitan meetings in a season, ensuring that she would easily defeat such accomplished male riders as Damien Oliver and Craig Williams, among many others, to the premiership.

The same report also noted that a day or two earlier, the Australian Olympic Committee had finalised its team for the

Tokyo Games, the biggest one ever sent abroad, and the second one to contain more women than men.

It had more Indigenous athletes, 16, than ever before, too, including basketballer Patty Mills who had been allocated the symbolic honour of being one of two flag-bearers at the opening ceremony alongside swimmer Cate Campbell.

These proved to be inspired decisions. The girls, in the pool and elsewhere, with Campbell their spiritual leader, provided the lion's share of the equal record 17 gold medals as well as seven silvers and 22 bronze, and Mills led his team brilliantly to their long-awaited medal of any colour, a treasured bronze.

The AOC's long-serving president, John Coates, has always been well aware that women have, on a pro-rata basis, been responsible for more of Australia's proud Olympic record than the blokes. Think Dawn Fraser, Betty Cuthbert, Susie O'Neill, Raelene Boyle, Shirley Strickland, Anna Meares, Cathy Freeman and Shane Gould, among many others — all of whom, just by the way, have always been fully appreciated in the media.

Coates promised years ago that the ratio would be adjusted, on merit of course, to reflect this and now he had delivered on it — with Barty enthusiastically joining in. She was a shock early exit from the singles but contributed to the medal tally with a bronze in the mixed doubles with John Peers, and was suitably proud of it.

In the *Herald Sun*, the eminent journalist Andrew Rule suggested that because she competes against men, Kah was now the greatest sportswoman in Australia, if not the world. It was not meant as any sort of put-down of Barty on the weekend of her finest moment, only that as with apples and oranges, it is impossible to make meaningful comparisons across the dividing lines of very different sports.

That's why it is futile to try to allocate a ranking spot for Barty's win on any list of the greatest Australian sporting feats of the last 10, 20, 50 or 100 years. It's just in the conversation — somewhere. Like beauty, it is in the eye of the beholder.

For what it's worth, when cyclist Cadel Evans became the first Australian to win the Tour de France in 2011, I wrote newspaper columns nominating it as the most impressive of this nation's many memorable triumphs for the half-century, roughly, that I had been watching sport for a living.

That was because Le Tour is the most physically and sometimes psychologically challenging assignment in mainstream sport on the planet, three weeks' worth of four-hour races almost every day, many of them requiring huge — and we do mean huge — mountains being climbed at a competitive pace.

It is about as far removed from whacking a tennis ball back and forth in a confined space as you can get — or steering a galloping horse for two minutes or so, for that matter — but that doesn't mean one is inherently superior or inferior to the other, only that elite sport comes in many forms, which is a very good thing.

Freeman's 400m win in Sydney is widely regarded as the gold-standard moment that most Australians can remember, but in reality that was more about circumstance — the enormous expectation confronting her, the massive emotional pressure — than the actual performance, as superb as that was. Her time of 49.11 seconds wasn't any sort of record or even a personal best — she had run faster at the previous Olympics, finishing second — and her conqueror on that occasion and still her most formidable rival, France's Marie-Jose Perec, was a late scratching.

None of which makes it any less impressive, only that it confirms there are often more ways than one of measuring and defining true sporting eminence, grandeur, majesty, call it what you will.

On the matter of reputational positioning, Barty's victory did settle one argument that seemed to annoy many of her fans, although there was never any evidence that it was causing her to lose any sleep.

Because she had hardly picked up a racquet throughout the lost year of 2020, while Osaka won the US Open and then the Australian Open at the start of 2021, giving her four majors in all, the validity of Barty's top ranking — and status as officially the world's best player — became the subject of some arch questions, some of which inferred she wasn't actually that good anyway regardless of what the scorebooks said.

But when she resumed, she won 29 of 34 matches in Australia, claiming tournaments in Melbourne, Miami and Stuttgart and making a final in Madrid, and when Osaka so controversially withdrew early in the French Open and all of

Wimbledon, the debate quickly lost its "legs".

By the time she bade farewell to the manicured lawns of London SW19, Barty had accumulated 9635 rankings points for the season to Osaka's 7336, a massive lead, had won 35 of her last 41 matches with four titles, and had been No. 1 for 84 weeks.

With Williams clearly on her last legs and no other obvious potentially dominant power emerging, Barty was clearly queen of all she surveyed, no argument about it.

In any case, she insists it is far from what matters most anyway. "I have nothing to prove," she has often said.

What does matter? Money? No. That doesn't seem to have ever been a crucial consideration, and while all professionals in any field need to get paid enough to survive while their careers are positioned for take-off, those days are a distant memory for her.

Her prizemoney for Wimbledon was $3.15m, which took her career earnings to $28,744,37m. According to one authoritative report, she also earns more than $4m annually from endorsements, making her the third highest paid female athlete behind Osaka and Williams. Her business partners are major brands, Jaguar, Kayo Sports, Head, Fila, Rado, Vegemite, Banana Boat and Esmi.

She pays tax in Australia, choosing to continue living where she always has in Ipswich, an urban but semi-rural area on the fringes of Brisbane, rather than basing herself in overseas havens such as the Bahamas or Bermuda as other Australian tennis players have. They say home is where the heart is, and it has never been truer than for her.

It all comes back to the true secret of her popularity, the values instilled as she grew up under the proud but prudent gaze of her parents, who supported her fully as her talent became evident and she pursued her dreams, never interrupting or interfering. They were acutely conscious of the difference between being good parents and incompetent coaches or managers and made no attempt to straddle the line.

In the Wimbledon washup, the importance of this was identified poignantly by another young star from another era when Jelena Dokic struggled to hold back tears as she paid tribute to Barty's parents.

## "I have nothing to prove"

Dokic, 38, was a "could be anything" prodigy when she made the Wimbledon quarter-finals as a 16-year-old in 2002 and rose to No. 4 in the world, despite her life being made an embarrassing misery by her Croatian father Damir, the epitome of the ugly parent syndrome that has scarred tennis and other sports far too often but which thankfully appears to be largely a thing of the past.

"I just want to get this out before I fall apart," she said, on TV, with tissues in her hand. "People underestimate the importance of family. She (Barty) talks about that all the time. As someone who didn't have that, it is so important. This will set an example to parents in Australia and around the world, not how to raise a champion but a genuinely wonderful human being. This is how you support them. You don't pressure them, you're there for them and this is why she's there. So a big shout-out to them. Well done."

As she spoke, Damir Dokic was languishing in a Serbian jail on assault charges. Happily, his daughter — now a prominent TV commentator — seems to have recovered her confidence, poise and mental health as she continues to make a living from the sport that threatened to swallow her up and spit her out through no fault of her own.

The stark comparison between her story and Barty's is an instruction manual for all families with kids who are gifted at sport — or anything else, for that matter.

The other comparison that has often been made, and continues to be, is with her contemporary on the men's side of the game, Nick Kyrgios.

The enigmatic Kyrgios, who is exactly a year minus three days older than Barty, probably was gifted with even more talent, certainly more flamboyance and flair, but has achieved far less, while his volatile and sometimes offensive behaviour has been the polar opposite.

While Barty has made the most of her gifts, Kyrgios has largely squandered his, much to the frustration — annoyance, even — of the sporting public, who see it almost as a dereliction of his national duty.

He doesn't, insisting that he doesn't really love the sport

and sees it only as a means to express himself and entertain others, with no real ambition to join the heavy hitters at the pointy end of the Grand Slam, even though he has proven he can beat them all, Roger Federer, Novak Djokovic and Rafael Nadal no exceptions.

Perhaps disingenuously, he insisted that "not everyone aspires to be like them," just before a typically two-toned appearance at Barty's Wimbledon, where he won two matches in impressive fashion before succumbing to an abdominal injury almost certainly caused by a failure to prepare properly.

There is a strong school of thought that this apparent mindset is, in fact, a convenient refuge for a deep-seated fear of failure — that if he professes not to care whether or not he wins, then he cannot be fairly criticised if he does not.

The truth is anyone's guess and although there remains ample time for him to get fair dinkum, to employ the Australian idiom, he seems destined to forever be eating Barty's dust as they navigate their respective journeys through life and sport. It seems unfortunate, but it's his choice and if he doesn't regret it then there is little point in the rest of us getting our knickers in a knot over it.

It does raise the highly debatable question of just how important it is to be popular as distinct from being successful, a point perhaps not lost on Djokovic, whose Wimbledon win, the 20th major of his stratospheric career, meant that he would almost certainly finish up as the undisputed best player in history — but far from the most liked, for whatever reasons. A temper tantrum when he found himself unable to win either the singles or doubles gold medals at the Olympics, and then forfeited the bronze medal match to Barty and Peers, leaving his own partner high, dry and frustrated, was another self-inflicted wound to his image.

Federer and Nadal, who also have 20 big wins, seem to have managed to combine both elements, as Barty has done.

With very few, if any, exceptions, Australia has always loved its tennis champions, possibly even more so than its cricketers, although that would be a very close-run thing.

In living memory, the starting point would be the great Frank Sedgman, winner of Wimbledon and three other majors and a constant hero of the Davis Cup, whose pleasant personality and scandal-free existence — now in his mid-nineties he is still married to virtually his first girlfriend and never drank alcohol in the early stages of his career — set the tone back in the 1950s, when discipline and dedication were the bywords of an era presided over by legendary coach Harry Hopman.

Sedgman was followed, among many others and in no particular order, by Rod Laver, Neale Fraser, Lew Hoad, Roy Emerson, Ken Rosewall, John Newcombe, Tony Roche and Pat Rafter — all of whom have enjoyed lofty reputations on and off the court, and not, of course, forgetting Lleyton Hewitt, who got off to a mixed start as a headstrong and unworldly teenager before maturing into a highly successful, unconditionally respected leader and role model.

Interestingly, while Court is far and away the most successful Australian player of either gender, her popularity has been damaged, to say the least, in recent years by her controversial religious beliefs, especially in relation to gender and sexuality issues. Her achievements can never be disrespected — they may never be surpassed — but suggesting that she is still a national hero is a sure way to quickly buy a national and international argument these days.

Although you have to be a so-called Baby Boomer, 70 or so years old, to have any active memory of Cawley — let alone Court, who mostly preceded her — she remains an enduring symbol of all that is good about Australian sport.

It will be a major surprise if that is not being said of Barty 50 years from now, if it does not become her essential legacy.

Because sport has such a heavy influence on Australia's culture and sense of national identity — especially as one generation follows another, as kids become adults and standards and expectations are formed and followed — that is a very welcome prospect. It is why Wimbledon 2021 will forever be high on posterity's recording of great moments in Australian sport.

2

# YOU CAN'T WIN 'EM ALL

Being Wimbledon champion — and the best player in the world, by a wide official margin — brings with it many benefits, not least confidence, belief and respect.

But there is one thing it doesn't and never will guarantee. It doesn't mean you can assume you'll automatically win the next match you play, let alone the next tournament, or that players who have never beaten you before will never do so in the future.

There is no such thing in elite sport as the right to rule, no matter how accomplished you might be.

That's not how it works, and being the grounded, realistic and self-aware character that she is, Ash Barty has never needed to have that explained to her.

Indeed, she saw fit to explain it to everyone else — or at least to her army of expectant fans — shortly after beginning her campaign at the last of the big four tournaments for 2021, the US Open.

"A massive part of our year is accepting that you don't win every single match and you're certainly not entitled to make big finals," she said.

If that wasn't the case, then winning the Grand Slam — all

four major tournaments in a calendar year — wouldn't be as diabolically difficult as it is, as even the likes of Serena Williams and Roger Federer will testify. No woman has done it since Germany's Steffi Graf in 1988.

However, Barty was riding so high after her historic triumph on the hallowed grasscourts of London — and with no obvious new superstar emerging, while her closest challenger Naomi Osaka was clearly unravelling psychologically — there was every reason for optimism that she could follow through by adding an Olympic gold medal and the US championship to her stellar year's work.

When you say it quickly like that, it sounds not just feasible, but logical, and eminently do-able.

In fact, it's hugely challenging, no matter who you are — the reality of which came into sharp focus when Novak Djokovic, with the Australian and French Opens and Wimbledon all safely locked away then failed to win a medal in singles, doubles or mixed doubles at the Tokyo Games, prompting a tantrum or two possibly because he believed himself entitled to the golden glory.

Barty didn't even make it through the first round, losing to Spain's Sara Sorribes Tormo, ranked 48 in the world, in a boilover. She settled for a bronze in the mixed doubles with John Peers, gifted by Djokovic forfeiting the match, leaving his bemused countrywoman Nina Stojonovic high and dry, and damaging his own controversial image some more.

Barty, of course, was just pleased and proud to contribute

to the national medal count, even at that lesser level, and wasn't about to beat herself up over not winning what she came for — because she didn't share Djokovic's sense of entitlement.

By this stage, everything about her progress was becoming more complicated than usual because she was being forced to live out of hotel rooms and suitcases for months on end, unable to go home for a circuit-breaker because quarantine rules in Australia made it pointless. Few, if any, players from other countries had to deal with that.

Unfazed, Barty bounced back to claim her fifth tournament of the year, in Cincinnati, without dropping a set, the perfect re-set to her momentum and mindset.

Even though she was the clear favourite to win, as she had been in Tokyo, the US Open was always going to be her most formidable assignment.

It always is for her — and Australian women in general. In the Open era, Margaret Court won it three times between 1969 and 1973 but since then only Sam Stosur, in 2011, has followed. In five previous attempts Barty has departed in the second, first, third, fourth and fourth rounds. It is the only major tournament in which she has not reached at least the semi-finals.

This time, she started well enough by beating Russian Vera Zvonareva and Danish 18-year-old Clara Tauson in straight sets, if not totally convincingly.

She didn't look to be completely on top of her game, and admitted as much, saying she had been "just chipping away —

the tennis hasn't been as clean as it was a couple of weeks ago, but we accept that. We keep working and go back to the practice court to try to rectify that."

That was when she started issuing subtle warnings about taking nothing for granted.

"Each and every round is a test," she said. "I don't come into this tournament with any expectation of myself to feel entitled to go deep or win the tournament or whatever.

"I just have to be prepared to play my best tennis. That's all I can ask from myself. Whether that's a first round or a final, my preparation and everything doesn't change."

Wimbledon, she said, was a long time ago.

"There's momentum in the sense of that one of my greatest goals was to win that tournament. I think playing and understanding how to win grand slams is very unique. Two weeks is a long time to be focused, have a bit of luck, stay healthy. I've learned the hard way that sometimes it doesn't go your way."

As usual, she proved to be on the money.

Other than her own underwhelming record at the New York showpiece, there was no real reason to believe that she would be proved right as quickly as she was.

Her third-round opponent, American Shelby Rogers, was a 28-year-old journey(wo)man, whose ranking hovers in the low forties, who had never been past the quarters at a slam. In five previous meetings, four of them in the preceding nine months, she had never prevailed. On paper it looked like a routine roadkill.

That was until Shelby — whose very occasional giant-killing exploits include wins over Simone Halep and Serena Williams — took the first set 6-1. Barty quickly levelled in the second, and then looked to be cruising home at 5-2 in the third when, without obvious warning, the sky fell in.

At that point, a Las Vegas bookmaker, Caesars Sportsbook, had Rogers at 5000-1 to win. Bookies do not usually display that level of generosity unless they are certain there is no way they can possibly lose. But in two-horse races, strange things do happen.

Barty twice served for the match but Shelby — to the roaring delight of the parochial New York crowd — forced a tie-breaker which she then won 7-5 with a minimum of anxious moments, unable to hold back tears as the shock denouement unfolded.

Barty had ... what, choked? That's possibly harsh, but not without an element of truth. Certainly, there are kinder words for it, but usually in these circumstances the correct and appropriate perspective is to give credit where it is due, and there is no doubt that Shelby deserves that. In her world, this was the definition of a famous victory, perhaps her best ever.

Barty never cries over spilt milk and this was certainly no exception.

The aftermath was as upbeat as it always is from her, win, lose or draw. And it was fully reciprocated, which was no surprise because they are close friends, the warmth of their embrace at the net an unmissable clue for anyone who might have been unaware of that.

Shelby echoed what Australian sports fans had been saying for at least a year or two and was probably speaking for most people in tennis.

"She is one of the most professional people I've ever met, as well as a good person, a funny individual," she said.

"Just refreshing to see. She's super down-to-earth. I mean she is one of my favourite people. Every time I lose to her, I can't be mad because she's such a nice person. It's like, man, she just kicked my butt. Then it's like, hey, you're going to find it one day.

"She's always encouraging to everyone around her. She brings up the energy wherever she goes.

"I can't say how much respect I have for her and what a great representative she is for women's tennis. I want to speak to what she's done this season. I think a lot of people are taking it for granted.

"She hasn't been able to go home since February, you guys. That's insane. This girl is everything every player wants to be." Barty, disappointed but not dejected and always the epitome of sportsmanship, couldn't have returned the compliment any more graciously.

"There are certain people on the tour that I think no matter what the result, you know you're always going to get a handshake, a smile, you're going to get that genuine respect. For me, Shelby has always been one of those people," she said.

"She's one that I most respect on tour, and she's an incredible person. She showed a lot of fight.

"I could see she was enjoying herself. I think that's the most important thing for both of us, we had a lot of fun out there.

"I know regardless of the result it never changes our relationship and that's really special when you've got someone who is just a class act on and off the court.

"It sucks in tennis that there's a winner and a loser every single day, but sometimes you don't mind losing to certain people. I think Shelby in her personality and her character, she's certainly one of those for me."

Not everybody knows how to turn defeat into a winner using words instead of a racquet but it's just another of Barty's well-honed skills. For her, it's always about much more than tennis.

3

# SEVEN STEPS TO GLORY: HOW ASH BARTY'S STARS ALIGNED AT WIMBLEDON

Ash Barty entered the Wimbledon fortnight at the end of June 2021 as World No. 1 in women's tennis. She had been No. 1 since mid-way through 2019.

She wasn't sure what her 2021 season would bring after being sidelined from competition for nearly a year through the COVID-19 pandemic ravaging the world.

Wimbledon, the Grand Slam held by the All England Lawn Tennis and Croquet Club, wasn't played in 2020 because of the COVID-19 pandemic, the same fate that befell many tournaments on the world circuit that year.

Commentators said Ash faced a tough time, likely to meet several highly ranked challengers as she moved through the draw chasing her dream.

There were also concerns about her fitness, arising from her withdrawal at Roland Garros, Paris, with a hip injury on 3 June, and from other niggles earlier in the year. Some may have even felt her demise in the fourth round of the 2019 version could weigh heavily on her.

But when she arrived at Wimbledon, there was no doubt she was ready.

"Straight after Paris, obviously there was some time where we needed to digest what was going on," she said. "We needed to get a full diagnosis. We were able to do that, which is a really crucial part of my rehab. We've been able to go through the rehab, do what we've needed to do, give ourselves the best chance to play here at Wimbledon.

"Now I feel like I'm fit, I'm ready to play, I'm excited to play. To have an opportunity to again play main draw here at Wimbledon is certainly something that excited me and really drove me to do everything as best as I possibly could with my team to make sure we're fit and we're here playing."

She was to answer any lingering questions in the most emphatic way possible.

## 26 JUNE, ROUND 1

Ash began against 32-year-old Carla Suarez Navarro (ESP), who boasted a career-high ranking of 6 and had been named in the Spanish team for the Tokyo Olympics.

The Spaniard's career was punctuated by illness; she successfully fought off cancer.

Ash was afforded Centre Court for her first round on the Tuesday, an honour traditionally reserved for the defending champion but injury to Simona Halep put Ash next in line.

She began strongly, taking the first set 6-1. She was a bit scratchy in the second set and lost 7-6 (1-7) in a tiebreaker. She regathered in the third to win it 6-1 and progress to the second round.

*HER PRESS CONFERENCE:*

"I think more than anything it was a great battle. I mean, in the game where I was trying to serve out the match, I just missed a few too many first serves and Carla was able to take the game on and hit some incredible returns. I think we just kind of accepted that and moved on.

"Again, she played a great tiebreak. She's a hell of a competitor, a hell of a fighter. It was a privilege to be able to share that moment, share that court with her. I hadn't had the opportunity to play Carla. It was really special to be able to experience what she can bring from the other side of the court.

"I think all credit goes to her for her resilience and her nature as a competitor, to be able to come back from the adversity that she has, and to be able to have that moment with her was nothing shy of remarkable."

## 29 JUNE, ROUND 2

Ash came up against Russian Anna Blinkova, three years her junior and ranked 89. She was relatively untroubled taking the Centre-Court match 6-4, 6-3, but conceded it hadn't been her best performance; 33 unforced errors (nine double faults) matched her number of winners.

*HER PRESS CONFERENCE:*

"A few things didn't feel quite right today. That's half the battle in sport, being able to find a way when it's not feeling all that great.

"I felt like when my back was against the wall today, I was able to bring the good stuff. It just wasn't quite there all the time. We have another opportunity to now go out on the practice court, work on it, try to bring some good stuff in the third round.

"Not my best serving day. But that happens as well. I felt like I was just out of rhythm a little bit. A few technical things weren't quite feeling spot on.

"But you have those days where some days you feel like you're eight-foot-tall and can't miss the box. Other days you feel like you're three-foot-nothing (and) just getting over the net is a bit of a battle.

"We just go back to work. Certainly nothing that will concern me over a longer period. We have those days. We just go back to kind of the routines that we usually would and try to find a way in the next match."

## 1 JULY, ROUND 3

Centre Court again, and Ash was drawn against 25-year-old Czech Katerina Siniakova, ranked 64 and fresh from a grass court final at Strasbourg just a week earlier. All went well for Ash until she served for the match at 5-4 in the second set. Her serve was broken but she quickly recovered and hit back to take the match 6-3, 7-5.

*HER PRESS CONFERENCE:*

"I've been very spoilt so far, enjoying absolutely every second I've been able to play on Centre Court. I think today's match was a little bit better again with the level. I felt like I was able to control more of the match and kind of bring it back to my patterns more often. I felt like I was able to use my serve effectively today.

"Overall happy with another solid performance. I feel like the consistency for me over the last couple of years, two years, not including 2020, has been good. It's been nice to be putting myself deeper into these tournaments.

"Each day it's a routine that we've been going through without a doubt to try to manage my body as best as possible. There have been some additional focuses that we've added, but nothing that's stressful or nothing that's concerning.

"I feel great. I feel excited to be in another round of 16, another second week of a Slam. Physically I feel good. I trust my body. I trust my game. It's about going out there and just trying to have fun."

## 3 JULY, ROUND OF 16

Ash faced a likely stiff test against 14th seed Czech Barbora Krejcikova who just weeks earlier had taken the French Open crown. It was Ash's first Wimbledon match away from Centre Court (on Court 1). She was in strife early, down 2-4 but called on her fighting qualities and great skills to stave off break points that would have put her down 2-5. She eventually took the first set 7-5, going on to seal the match 6-3 in the second set.

*HER PRESS CONFERENCE:*

"There was certainly no lack of preparation. It was a different preparation. Without a doubt it was unique. I did everything in my power to make sure I was well-prepared to come into this tournament. I feel like we're doing all the right things, we're trying to do everything that we can each and every day to be as ready as possible for the next day. That's no different to how we prepare for each and every tournament.

"I feel good. I have an incredible team. I have a great physio, I have a great trainer, a great coach. We're all very much on the same wavelength when it comes to how we want to plan, how we want to prepare. Also a little bit of luck. You need things to go your way.

"The rehab for me in between Paris and playing here at Wimbledon was as best as we could hope for. But I feel great. I feel like each and every day we continue to do the right recoveries, we try to prepare in a way knowing I can give myself the best chance to walk out on court to play at absolutely a hundred per cent and I feel great.

"The focus in between matches is exactly how it always is. It's recovery and prioritising that recovery. Always been a massive part of my career. Being able to do that this week has been great.

"We just continue to do all the right things. Obviously, like

I've said, the rehabs between Paris and here in London, we had 22 or 23 days. We were able to kind of work backwards from that point. We did everything as best we could.

"I'm feeling great. I'm feeling ready. Obviously getting more and more matches is really nice to be able to feel the court under my feet."

## 6 JULY, QUARTER-FINAL

Ash could have felt a little uncomfortable as she faced Australia's No. 2 player, 28-year-old Ajla Tomljanovic, whose career-high ranking had been 39 and was going into her first Grand Slam quarter-final. But Ash showed no mercy, her sometimes unplayable slice and 17 top-spin forehand winners powering her to a 6-1, 6-3 victory.

*HER PRESS CONFERENCE:*

"This is my dream. I'm in an extremely fortunate position that I'm getting to do what I love, getting to do what I dreamt as a kid. So I think I've just got a whole lot of gratitude for the fact that I get to come out here and do what I love.

"The world, the way we're living at the moment, I think it's incredible that we're able to play, compete, have people enjoy it with us. So I'm certainly enjoying every single minute that I get out on those courts.

"Something that I wanted to do is to start well. But also not making a massive, massive emphasis on the start, allowing myself to not panic if things didn't start overly well.

"It was just working my way in, like we always do, not putting any more emphasis on any point or any situation. It just kind of is what it is. Each and every one, I just wanted to try and play as well as I could with as much clarity and freedom as I could.

"I think each and every opportunity I get to play, I learn. I take it for what it is. I can't do any more than that. I can't think too far ahead or worry about what has happened in the past. It's about focusing on the present moment and the opportunity that I've got. That's all I do.

"The clay season was quite long. As for the grass season for me, it's one tournament, pretty cut-throat. I think it's allowing myself time to feel relaxed on the court, to learn about the surface, to continue to kind of find my rhythm and find my groove on the grass.

"But I think today I was able to use my weapons a little bit better and just bring the ball back into my patterns a bit more regularly. I certainly wasn't as loose as I have been with errors and kind of ill-timed lapses, I suppose. But I felt really sharp today. I felt like I knew I needed to bring that level in order to match it with Ajla."

## 8 JULY, SEMI-FINAL

Angelique Kerber loomed as a serious challenge to "the dream". The German, though ranked 28 and seeded 25, boasted three grand slam victories (including Wimbledon in 2018) and a

World No. 1 ranking during her career.

Her ranking as she entered the semi-final belied her big-match abilities and Ash was expecting a tough contest, describing it as her "ultimate test". The first set went according to plan for Ash, taking it 6-3. But the fightback came and Kerber took the second 7-6 (7-4 in a tie-breaker) after going up 5-2. As she had done previously, Ash regathered and sealed the match 6-3 in the third and headed off into her long-awaited dream of the Wimbledon final.

*HER PRESS CONFERENCE:*

"I have a very large team. I know not everyone is here with me this week. I've got obviously my family at home, I mean, trainers, physios back in Australia. I also have my trainer and physio this week as well as Tyz (coach) and Garry (partner).

"It's nice to be able to share some of these awesome moments with those that put so much time and energy into my career and allow me, encourage me, help me kind of work and figure out a plan and a way that they try and achieve our dreams. I think being able to share that with them is really special.

"That match was a great level, the best level I've played, in quite some time. I think Angie is an incredible competitor. She brought out the best in me today. I think being able to challenge myself against a champion like her, it was just nice to play a really good level throughout the whole match, kind of fought and scrapped when I had to, controlled the ball when I had to. But being able to have that feeling on the last point was amazing.

"I think it's all about the moment, it's all about taking it in, it's about enjoying it. I think when you're playing in a big match like that, of course there's a lot on the line. It's also very easy for me to fall back on the fact that this is a game of tennis.

"There are obviously so many things that I do, and kind of I work so hard behind the scenes with my team to try to put myself in these moments, but it's also really important to enjoy the moments.

"I think I was really able to enjoy myself today right from the start. I had a lot of fun. That was a focus of mine. I wanted to go out there and enjoy playing against Angie in such an incredible moment, and regardless of the result, walk off the court knowing that I enjoyed it, I had fun, and I kind of gave it a crack and gave it my all. That's all that I was going to ask of myself today. To be able to bring a level of tennis like I did was kind of the cherry on top.

"I think being able to have an opportunity to play in a final here at Wimbledon is incredible."

## 10 JULY, THE CHAMPIONSHIP

No. 8 seed and world No. 13 Karolina Pliskova of the Czech Republic was always going to be a tough opponent, Ash's 5-2 lead in their seven previous encounters meaning little on Centre Court of Wimbledon on the Saturday night.

Pliskova was world No. 1 for eight weeks in 2017.

Commentators highlighted her serve — pacey, powerful and usually precise. She was renowned for her high first-serve percentages and ability to serve aces. Her first serve speed averaged 175 km/h. She was also strong on the forehand.

How would Ash cope with that?

Her game had been built on her ability to get to the net, hitting volleys to win points. Her backhand slice was always a go-to shot when the chance presented, able to keep the ball low to force errors from opponents. But her biggest attribute was court sense, being able to anticipate and adjust quickly.

There would have been some nerves, both players in their first Wimbledon final.

Pliskova survived a three-set battle against second seed Aryna Sabalenka for a 5-7, 6-4, 6-4 victory to get to the final.

Having won three titles already in 2021 (in Australia, Miami and Stuttgart) Ash was in peak form for Wimbledon, despite the injury setback in France.

Ash fired out of the blocks in the first set, capitalising on a nervous start by Pliskova to race to a 4-0 lead.

Pliskova managed to recover but Ash took the first set 6-3.

By the second set, Pliskova was on the way back. Even though Ash served for the second set and the match at 6-5 up, the Czech player wasn't giving in. She broke Ash who served a rare double-fault to force the set into a tie-breaker that the Czech clinched 7-6 (7-4) to set up a dramatic final set.

But just as she has always seemed able to do whenever a

match got tight, Ash steadied.

She took a 3-0 lead straight away before surviving another tense moment or two trying to close it out when 5-3 up, eventually sealing it 6-3. Her first serve problems (54% in and 61% won) were negated by Pliskova's unforced errors.

Ash shaded Pliskova in most aspects of the game. Pliskova won more points at the net, but Ash won 88 points to her opponent's 78 and had three more winners and three fewer unforced errors. It was Ash's 187th career victory (71 losses).

The coveted Wimbledon Venus Rosewater Dish was Ash's, 6-3, 6-7, 6-3.

"This is incredible," Ash said as she savoured the moment on Centre Court. "It took me a long time to verbalise the fact that I wanted to dare to dream and say I wanted to win this incredible tournament and being able to live out my dream right now with everyone here has made it better than I could ever imagine.

"I didn't sleep a lot last night, I was thinking of all the what-ifs, but I think when I was coming out on this court I felt at home in a way.

"To be able to share that with everyone here and share that with my team is incredible. It was the most incredible feeling I think I've ever experienced on a tennis court. There was certainly disbelief. I've worked so hard my whole career with my team and with people that mean the most to me to try and achieve my goals and my dreams."

## TOUCH AND GO

Ash revealed a little more about the injury she aggravated in Paris and how it nearly ended her Wimbledon ambitions.

Her team, headed by coach Craig Tyzzer, kept the bad news from her that her injury could keep her out until August.

"They kept a lot of cards close to their chest and didn't tell me a lot of the odds, didn't tell me a lot of the information that they'd got from other specialists," Ash said. "I think them not telling me that just proved how much we were up against the odds.

"There weren't too many radiologists in Australia who had seen my injury. In a sense, it was a two-month injury. Being able to play here at Wimbledon was nothing short of a miracle.

"I think now to be playing pain-free through this event was incredible. It's funny, sometimes the stars align. You can think positively, you can plan, and sometimes the stars do align, you can chase after your dreams."

Ash said she realised getting to the first round of Wimbledon could be "touch and go".

"I'm a firm believer in everything happens for a reason, the good moments and the tough moments," she said. "I felt like I was able to get better and better with each match and trust myself more and more each and every time I stood out on the court. Some of my toughest moments have come at Wimbledon. Now some of my most incredible moments have come here as well.

"I think it's just an iconic venue. It's an amazing club. To be able to learn so much from this place, I think I'm a very lucky girl."

She didn't forget her fans back home: "I know they're at home watching. I miss them, I love them. I'm so glad that they were able to at least watch and share this with me. But I can't wait to get home to them in a few months' time and really celebrate," she said.

Karolina Pliskova also felt the emotion of the moment, after losing a grand slam final for the second time — the other the 2016 US Open, in three sets, to Angelique Kerber.

"Thank you so much, I enjoy every minute to play on this court," Pliskova said as tears welled in her eyes. "I think Ash played an incredible tournament and an incredible match today."

Three Australian tennis icons were lavish in their praise for the country's new Wimbledon champion.

Leading the way was Evonne Goolagong Cawley, whose path Ash trod on the way to glory.

She said: "Ash to me is like a little sister and part of my family. I think we treat each other that way. It's amazing that she won her first Grand Slam at the French. That was my first Grand Slam. That same year, I won Wimbledon in 1971. It was such a thrill for me because I achieved my dream."

Sometimes described as her mentor, and certainly an inspiration to Ash, Goolagong Cawley whose feats at Paris and Wimbledon she emulated, said: "She was 13 and after I saw her in a match, I knew she had all the skills — the slice, the volley, the smash, everything in one game. I looked at Roger (husband

Roger Cawley) and we thought 'She's got it, she's going to be a champion.' So look at her now."

Two others, both Queenslanders and both past Wimbledon singles champions, weighed in. Rod Laver said: "She's something special, she doesn't worry at all. She just goes out there and plays." Roy Emerson agreed: "She's got her head together. You see her play and you can't tell if she's winning or losing. She just gets on with it and that makes her a tough opponent."

Next stop: Tokyo and the Olympics. But would there be a letdown after the magic moment at Wimbledon?

"I certainly have no fears about my fitness. Of course, some things will happen, that's the life of being an athlete. But I know that I've got the very best team around me to prepare me in a way as best as we can," Ash said.

Results at the Olympics would have no bearing on Ash's ranking; there was no prizemoney on offer and no rankings points at stake.

Ash had accrued 9,635 rankings points after her Wimbledon win, 2,299 clear of her nearest rival, Naomi Osaka, but she lost some points by skipping the Montreal tournament yet went into the Cincinnati tournament on 16 August still with a comfortable lead.

Regardless of the outcome in Cincinnati Ash would still be heading into the US Open on top of the rankings.

*Press conference coverage from asapsports.com.*

## A BRONZED AUSSIE

Ash Barty bowed out of the Olympics women's tennis singles in the first round. Novak Djokovic bowed out of the gold medal hunt with a loss in the men's singles semi-finals.

The two world No. 1s went to Tokyo to win medals. Only Ash Barty came away with one.

It was several weeks later, at the Cincinnati WTA tournament that Ash was able to analyse what happened in Tokyo.

She conceded she had been struggling with mental fatigue since her Wimbledon victory, probably explaining her disappointing performance in Tokyo.

"It was probably the strangest feeling of my life in those days after winning Wimbledon," she said in a WTA interview.

There are plenty of people who questioned why tennis and golf were in the Olympics. Why do these superstar players take part? It's not prizemoney (there is none). It's not rankings points (there are none). One of the arguments against their significance is that golfers and tennis players contest many major events, sometimes several times in a year, the Slams and Opens (majors) and various season-ending prizemoney bonanzas, whereas as some Olympians only get one shot at glory — an Olympic medal available every four years (usually).

For most Olympians the desire is to compete for their country, wearing their country's colours. Medals, too, are a part of personal ambition.

Ash explained her motivation: "I think making your first

Olympic team, particularly as an Australian, we have such a rich history and the Olympics is something I've always dreamt of and obviously super excited to get out there and represent the green and gold with the rest of the team. It's a massive, united team and I can't wait to be a part of it.

"Competing in an Olympic Games is always a dream, as young kids you aspire to it, and I think we have so many iconic legends in Australian sport who have paved the way for us. Now for me to get a chance to create my own legacy, my own guide for youngsters coming through is really exciting.

"I'm excited to play both singles and doubles. Any opportunity you get to wear the green and gold, I wanted to grab it with both hands. I'm fit, I'm healthy, I'm excited to play doubles with Storm (Sanders), she's a childhood friend and we've played a lot together from when we were young. So to be able to live out this dream with her is really, really special."

Asked if she could win gold, Ash said: "I'll give it a crack, like everyone else will be, but I'll certainly be giving it my all."

She didn't get the gold.

She bowed out in a shock first round result in the singles and she and Storm (ranked 6) bowed out of the doubles in the quarter-finals.

That left her and John Peers to try for a medal in the mixed doubles. They had a "good crack" and reached the semi-finals.

A loss in the semi-finals meant they were to play off for the bronze medal against Serb pair Novak Djokovic and Nina

Stojanovic, who had also lost their quarter-final.

But men's No. 1 Djokovic couldn't take part, citing an injured shoulder and maybe some other niggles which he said also put him in some doubt for the coming American events. Earlier he'd lost his singles semi-final, a result with which he definitely was not pleased.

So, the bronze medal went to Ash and John Peers in a walkover.

That may not have been the medal fans envisaged but Ash and John Peters were excited with the result. Their medal was just Australia's sixth Olympic medal in tennis; the first since Alicia Molik won bronze in the women's singles at Athens in 2004.

"It has been a long time since a tennis team has brought home a medal for the Australian public and our country. It is exciting for us. We're rapt and we're going to enjoy tonight, enjoy tomorrow and soak it in over the next 24 to 48 hours," Ash said.

"This was a tournament, an event we really earmarked at the start of the year wanting to do well," she added. "To share this moment with Johnny and both our families back home is incredible. I think we enjoy this one then reset and get ready for the American hardcourt season."

Like most Olympic events of Tokyo 2020 (delayed until 2021 because of the pandemic), the lack of spectators may have worked against some of the tennis players, especially those who thrive on crowd involvement and partisan support.

## SINGLES

Fans were shocked when Ash was eliminated from the women's Olympic singles championship in the first round, particularly coming in fresh from the Wimbledon championship. She was in sparkling form in the first round of doubles the previous day.

But 24-year-old Spaniard Sara Sorribes Tormo, ranked 47, wasn't going to be a push-over and ended Ash's singles medal dream in straight sets 6-4, 6-3.

Ash showed a glimpse of a possible comeback when she recovered from an early service break in the second set, but the Spaniard stayed ahead with another break in the seventh game. A fifth break sealed Ash's fate.

Ash seemed off the pace from the start and didn't really get into the match, losing two of her first three service games and making 55 unforced errors in two sets, a huge advantage for the Spaniard.

"It was just loose," Ash said. "I really wanted to take the match on here today. Just too erratic today. Wasn't able to make enough balls.

"I never really felt comfortable out there and wasn't able to play the match on my terms. The key to my game is serving well and I wasn't able to do that today. I was a bit erratic and made too many errors," she said.

Was the oppressive heat a factor?

"It's brutal. Like an Australian summer," Ash said. "I enjoy the heat and love playing out here in these conditions. Wasn't meant to be."

Ash's loss wasn't the only upset in the women's singles; home favourite and likely challenger to Ash's No. 1 ranking Naomi Osaka was bundled out of the singles in the second round.

Belinda Bencic of Switzerland won the gold medal, Markéta Vondroušová of the Czech Republic the silver and Elina Svitolina of Ukraine the bronze. The Olympic Games tennis was an International Tennis Federation event, and results had no bearing on WTA standings.

## DOUBLES

Ash joined 26-year-old Storm Sanders from Rockhampton, Queensland, for Australia's tilt at the women's doubles. They had played some doubles together previously, mostly as juniors. Storm was in the best form of her career, having reached the women's singles quarter-finals and the doubles semi-finals at Wimbledon with American Caroline Dolehide. The Australians were seeded 6 at Tokyo.

They took the court with fewer than 10 spectators on day one of tennis competition on 24 July for their first-round clash against Japanese pair, Makoto Ninomiya and Nao Hibino.

The Australians breezed through the opening match 6-0, 6-1 in 50 minutes, Ash giving her fans hope of what might be to come in the singles the next day.

She showed a lot of her skills, particularly court management and return of serve; she seemed to have lost little since Wimbledon by way of determination to do her best.

"Playing with my childhood friend in what is a dream for both of us is really cool. And to be here in some of the most unique circumstances I think ever for an Olympic Games, it's really awesome for us," Ash said.

"We're very grateful and thankful that we're able to be here to play and to experience what is really a cool Games."

Tougher matches were ahead.

Their second-round clash against Chinese pair Zhaoxuan Yang and Yifan Xu was tighter, although the Australians seemed to have a bit in reserve winning 6-4, 6-4. There were some questions about how Ash would hit back after her shock loss in the first-round singles, but she showed few signs of a letdown. As well, Storm Sanders seemed to lift, complementing Ash's solid game.

The win took them into the quarter-finals against the top seeds, Barbora Krejcikova and Katerina Siniakova of the Czech Republic.

But that's where their run came to an end.

The Australians took control of the match early, racing to a 4-1 lead and securing the opening set in 24 minutes. But the more experienced top seeds came back to take the second and clinched the match in the tiebreaker, 3-6, 6-4, 10-7 (deciding sets being the first to 10 points, 2 clear).

## MIXED DOUBLES

Ash and Victorian John Peers had previous mixed doubles experience with reasonable success, making it to the quarter-finals at Wimbledon in 2013 and the US Open in 2014.

It took Ash and Peers just 71 minutes to overcome Argentines Horacio Zeballos and Nadia Podoroska 6-1, 7-6 in the first round and earn a place in the quarter-finals.

Next, they faced second seeds Stefanos Tsitsipas and Maria Sakkari of Greece. The Australians overcame the more fancied pair in a hard-fought 6-4, 4-6, 10-6 victory.

The Greek pair were both top-20 singles players and proved a strong doubles combination, having represented Greece at the Hopman Cup in 2019.

At a set apiece, the first-to-10 tiebreak was used. Ash and Peters produced some of their best tennis to slip to a 7-3 lead and complete an impressive victory for a shot at a medal match, becoming the first Australian team to advance to an Olympic mixed doubles semi-final.

Victory in the semi-final would have meant a play-off for gold or silver and a loss meant a play-off for bronze.

The semi-final was a tight contest, but Ash and Peers (unseeded) were unable to get the better of Anastasia Pavlyuchenkova and Andrey Rublev (seeded 4) representing the Russian Olympic Committee after Russian athletes were not permitted to compete as team Russia.

The Australians took the first set 7-5, lost the next 4-6

and came within a shout of taking the tiebreaker before going down 11-13.

The loss was to pit the Australians against Serbs Novak Djokovic and Nina Stojanovic for the bronze medal, the world No. 1s in women's and men's tennis against each other.

But Djokovic could not take the court and the walkover meant the Australians were bronze medallists.

Anastasia Pavlyuchenkova and Andrew Roblev took the gold medal over compatriots Elena Vesnina and Aslan Karatsev (silver).

Ash was in no doubt she and Peers were worthy bronze medallists.

"We obviously wanted to have the challenge of playing one of the best nations in the world. But regardless of whether we got on the court or not, I feel we deserved it. We definitely deserved to be in the bronze medal match," she said.

Summing up her Olympic campaign, Ash said: "No matter what format, singles, doubles or mixed, I came here with a focus to win a medal for our nation. We played incredible tennis this week, it was a unique circumstance to win the bronze, but we deserved it.

"For me, being my first experience (at the Olympics), it is quite remarkable. We did not want to make up the numbers. We wanted to win a medal for our country.

"To be able to contribute to our medal count is really exciting. A massive highlight of my career being able to call myself an Olympian and a medallist."

Ash sent her bronze medal home with an Olympics team physio to pass it on to her parents, Josie and Robert. She had a trip to the US next stop on her itinerary.

## ENJOYING THE MOMENT IN TEAM OZ

The Olympic experience obviously left an impression on Ash. At her press conference before her first tournament in the US at Cincinnati, she spoke enthusiastically about her time in Tokyo.

"That whole Olympic experience, being able to see a few Aussies I hadn't seen since January, February, was incredible," she said.

"And obviously to be able to share some of our stories we've had over the last three, four months, being able to talk through them and kind of chat to them about it and just hear some Aussie accents made a massive difference.

"Being around so many other Aussies just created this incredible feeling of home and normalcy, I suppose. That was really refreshing. That was really nice.

"I think Aussies have this incredible ability of creating an equal playing field, everyone is equal. And I think at Aussie headquarters in the Village, there was a really strong sense of that."

What about Paris in 2024? Ash was non-committal but certainly left the door open for another shot as she spoke about the "vibe."

"Even though all of the athletes, all of us, we weren't able to go (to) all of the sports, it created an incredible vibe at our

Australian headquarters," she said.

"Everyone was wrapped around the TVs, everyone was watching, supporting, and it almost brought us together more in the fact that we only had one place where we could watch everyone.

"It almost dragged us all there, and the vibe was pretty good."

## THE NORTH AMERICAN HARD-COURT SWING

"There are no certainties in sport, no certainties in tennis. It's just about playing each and every day as best you can as they come and not focusing or concerning yourself or your self-worth with results." — Ash on her way to Flushing Meadows, August 2021.

Ash turned up for the US Open at the Western and Southern Open in Cincinnati, blowing away the competition to become the first Australian champion there since her mentor Evonne Goolagong Cawley in 1973.

There was another record she took to Cincinnati — 14 of her most recent matches went to three sets. But each time she dropped a set, she was able to recover and close out victory.

There was no such issue this time. Ash didn't drop a set as she dominated the week-long tournament, playing on five successive days and improving in each match. She defeated three major champions along the way — Victoria Azarenka, Barbora Krejcikova and Angelique Kerber.

She said afterwards she had been at something of a loss after the Olympics.

"It was probably the strangest feeling of my life in those days after winning Wimbledon. I kind of wasn't sure what I should be doing. I didn't know what to do," she told WTA Insider.

"It certainly took a little bit longer. I felt like I still had a lot of fatigue in Tokyo. I had a lot of fatigue the last two weeks. Even at the start of this week, I was a little bit unsure of what my tennis was going to be like, purely from a mental and emotional standpoint.

"But being able to kind of scrap through practice and trust myself, knowing that, give yourself a chance to play, give yourself a chance to work into the tournament and you'll kind of find it. I think we've been able to do that this week again."

She did find "it", going all the way to the Cincinnati final where she defeated wild card entrant and No. 76 ranked Jil Teichmann (Switzerland) 6-3, 6-1 to claim her 13th career WTA singles title.

Teichmann claimed some big scalps on her way to the final including World No. 1 contenders Naomi Osaka and Karolina Pliskova, as well as Olympic champion Belinda Bencic. Ash was a scalp too far away.

Ash expressed some reservations when she arrived in Cincinnati in mid-August: "This is a place where I've never quite felt 100 per cent comfortable," she said. "But we've got New York right around the corner. This period of the year is always an enjoyable one, I can't wait to get started back into some matches again."

She need not have worried; after a first round bye afforded to the top seed, she went on to account for British qualifier Heather Watson 6-4, 7-6; Victoria Azarenka (Belarus) 6-0, 6-2; Barbora Krejcikova (Czech) 6-2, 6-4; and Angela Kerber (Germany) 6-2, 7-5.

German Angelique Kerber is well-placed to assess Ash's abilities — she lost to her in semi-finals at Wimbledon and Cincinnati.

Kerber said: "You know, I think she has so much confidence right now. She plays so well, and she served good. I think this is also a big weapon from her. You know, she's just playing really like tricky, as well.

"She knows where to put the ball and how to play in the moments where it's really important. So I think the whole game of hers is really tough, and, you know, that's why she's there where she is."

After her Cincinnati victory, Ash made a gesture hardly even seen on the tour. She called her team, including boyfriend Garry Kissick and coach Craig Tyzzer, to share her moment of glory on court for the trophy presentation.

Victory in the final gave her a fifth singles tournament title for the year after the Yarra Valley Classic in Melbourne and Miami, Stuttgart, Madrid and Wimbledon titles. That was one more win than her breakout year in 2019. Her record against Top 20 opponents for the year stood at 14-1. She also became the first player to win 40 matches for the year and headed off to New

York having been the world No. 1 for 83 successive weeks and 90 weeks overall. Her record in finals for the year was now 5-1, losing only to Aryna Sabalenka (Belarus) in Madrid.

Some other notable stats after Cincinnati: Ash led the WTA in 2021 in first serve points percentage won and total serve points percentage won. She also had the best break points saved percentage of players with at least three matches played, had the best service games won percentage of players with at least three matches played and the leading first serve return points won percentage of any player in the top 10.

Perhaps more significantly, she extended her lead in world ranking points to more than 3,000 over Aryna Sabalenka (Belarus) and more than 3,400 over defending US Open champion Naomi Osaka (Japan) who both were bundled out of the Cincinnati tournament in early rounds, with Sabalenka moving to No. 2 due to Osaka not being able to defend all her points from the previous year.

Ash also increased her lead in the Porsche Race to the WTA Finals, transferred for 2021 to Guadalajara, Mexico, from Shenzhen (China) where she won in 2019 (the series wasn't held in 2020). It still looked like Ash might need a bigger garage for another Porsche, the prize for the leading pointscorer in the "race" by the time the elite (top) eight players arrived in Mexico for the play-offs at year's end. The finals were slated to return to Shenzhen in 2022.

"I think being able to come through and play a really clean

week and walk away with the title is probably not what I really expected of myself, but (it's) certainly nice," Ash said after the match in which she fired eight aces and broke Teichmann five times, facing just two break points herself.

The US Open was the only Slam in which Ash hadn't reached a singles semi-final; in fact, she had not progressed past the fourth round at Flushing Meadows. Her best results were the last 16 in 2018 and 2019. An extra challenge in 2021 was to win back-to-back Grand Slams.

"Each time we've played here in New York I've felt like I've played well," she said. "I just haven't been able to quite get over that hurdle of the fourth round. This year's no different. We try and do the right things right from the start and try and put ourselves in a position where we can go deep in the tournament."

The Cincinnati tournament was extremely important in Ash's preparations for the US Open after the disappointment of Tokyo. There were also some questions about the effect of being away from home for much of 2021.

"I think there was probably a part of me that was a little bit unsure of how this year would go for a couple of reasons," she said in a WTA interview.

"One being seven to eight months out of the tour last year, and two, being in a completely new adventure, a new scenario, a new feeling for me of being away from home for so long.

"We were going to have to find ways to re-energise. We were going to have to prioritise weeks. That was going to be a massive part of our year, was scheduling correctly to make sure that we felt like we could peak at the right times.

"Whether we actually got the result is irrelevant. But actually to understand me as a human, before the athlete, and making sure that I was fresh for the big moments.

"I've played a lot of tennis, I've played a lot of matches, and there haven't been too many where I've come off the court and been disappointed with the output, which is all that I can ask."

The US Open was again to test her mettle.

## FALLING SHORT

Ash's result in the 2021 US Open was something of a boilover, a shock, crashing out at the hands of 40th ranked American Shelby Rogers in the round of 32 and again failing to reach the quarter-finals.

Twice she was unable to capitalise on a double-break and serve out for victory at 5-2 and 5-4 in the deciding set, Rogers claiming probably her biggest scalp 6-2, 1-6, 7-6 (7-5) in just on two hours. There was no recovery to win a decider this time.

"Yeah, tough one. It's never nice when you have a couple opportunities to serve out a match and can't get it done," Ash said.

"It's a tough one to swallow. But it is what it is tonight. I found a way back into my match. I found a way to really turn it in my favour and just wasn't able to just quite finish off. It's disappointing but we'll move on."

The 28-year-old Rogers, never ranked higher than 40th, reaching that in July 2021 had just two Grand Slam quarter-finals in her record. The Barty party at Flushing Meadows had foundered, after a promising start where she won her first three matches without dropping a set and looking likely to progress to the round of finals for the first time. It wasn't to be.

Regardless, Ash left New York as the WTA's No.1 player for the 86th consecutive week and 92nd week overall. None of the remaining contenders were in reach of her big lead in the ranking points. Her nearest rival, Aryna Sabalenka (Belarus) could only get within about 1,100 points even if she won the US Open. Sabalenka didn't reach the final, which was fought out by two teenagers — Brit Emma Raducanu defeating Canadian Leylah Fernandez in straight sets and becoming the first qualifier to win a Slam.

The loss must have stung. But Ash, as usual was philosophical: "I think there are a few things tonight I'm happy to accept," she said. "There are some things I'm disappointed in, without a doubt. In the end, I just didn't quite have enough in the tank. I've left everything out on the court this year. It was no different tonight. I just didn't quite have enough to get over the line, which is disappointing but we move on. I sleep well tonight knowing I gave everything I could; it just wasn't quite enough."

Ash went into the US Open, the last of the season's Slams, with an impressive record — a 40-7 match winning record and having lost only one of her previous 10 matches for five titles including Wimbledon, and a 25-3 record on American hard courts since 2019.

## UP FOR THE CHALLENGE

How was Ash feeling as she launched her US Open challenge? "I've played a lot of tennis, I've played a lot of matches, and there haven't been too many where I've come off the court and been disappointed with the output, which is all that I can ask," she told WTA Tour.

"It's irrelevant whether I win matches or titles. I certainly know that, in all for maybe one or not even two matches this year, have I been disappointed with my output. That's all I can ask of myself.

"Having that accountability on me, that I want to bring that every single day, has made the year more fun, has almost forced myself to play better tennis and therefore win more matches. I think being able to put myself in that big situation more and more times has been really exciting."

There were a couple of notes of caution. She hadn't made any final there in five appearances; her best were in 2018 and 2019 when she reached the round of 16. Also, it had been five years since a woman finished a year with two Grand Slam titles (Angela Kerber was the last in 2016).

And of course, former World No. 1 Naomi Osaka was probably waiting for Ash as the two halves of the women's draw came together late in the tournament. Sadly, the clash with the defending US Open champion and 2021 Australian Open champion didn't eventuate.

Osaka, who had been battling mental health issues and only played less than half the matches of Ash and other top contenders during the year was bundled out in three sets by Canadian teenager Leylah Fernandez in the third round after losing her composure on court.

One threat was gone, but that was of no consequence as it turned out.

It was Ash's first entry into the US Open as World No. 1. Her first-round assignment, (no first round bye for top seeds) on Centre Court (Arthur Ashe Stadium) was tricky. She faced Russian Vera Zvonareva for the first time in her career. Ash was quickly off the mark, display her best tennis to breeze through the first set 6-1.

Ash sent down 11 aces in, including a Tour-topping 300th for the year — she was averaging six aces a match at that point and hit 31 winners. The second set was tougher and she faced break point before closing it out.

Ash had to battle hard to get past Zvonareva, failing to serve out the match when leading 5-4 with Zvonareva breaking back when Ash served a double-fault. At 6-6 the set progressed to a tiebreaker in which the Russian at one stage held set point. But Ash held on to take it 9-7 to and seal the match in straight sets, 6-1, 7-6, over and hour and 28 minutes.

In the second round, she was opposed to Danish teenager Clara Tauson, who had won a WTA 250 tournament at Chicago the previous week and was ranked 78. The pair had not played each other before.

The match progressed along similar lines to that in the first round: Ash blitzed her opponent in the first set and staved off break points to take a tighter second set, for a 6-1, 7-5 victory.

Ash's heavy slice backhand was a significant problem for the Dane who struggled to deal with the low shooting ball.

"My tactic is to bring in the slice as much as possible," she said. "It doesn't work every time but over time that repetitive motion making your opponent have to get down and reach the ball is effective."

Against a backdrop of chaos caused by Hurricane Ida in New York, Ash maintained her composure to see off the younger and taller challenger for her 14th successive WTA tour victory.

"The storm was pretty devastating and I was just trying to grasp what was happening here and hoping people from the site were able to get home safely," she said afterwards.

She was just one win away from going into the last 16 and a possible crack at the round of finals.

But Shelby Rogers ended the dream.

Rogers put the writing on the wall in their Round of 32 clash when she swept Ash aside 6-2 in the first set, highlighted by Ash's high number of unforced errors and low first-serve percentage.

Ash dug deep to claim the second in convincing style, 6-1, setting up an epic deciding third-set.

Commentators had expressed some reservations about Ash's ability to serve out a match sometimes. Did they have a point?

Ash served for the match twice in the third set but came up short as the dogged Rogers fought back to force a tie-breaker that the American eventually won the decider 7-5 to clinch the third set.

Rogers, the last American left in the women's draw, had been 0-6 in her career against top-seeded players.

She said the return of spectators to the US Open played a role in her upset victory. No fans were allowed to attend the tournament the previous year ago because of the pandemic.

"The crowd is next-level this year," Rogers told the fans. "You've picked who you want to win, so thank you for picking me tonight."

Commentators noted Ash looked "flustered" in the first set with unforced errors costing her dearly.

The fightback in the second set was always on the cards but the third set saw Rogers emerge with new determination, buoyed by the home crowd support.

Asked how she could explain this fightback to secure her first ever win over the Australian, Rogers said: "I'm not sure I can. She took me down twice in Australia in front of her home crowd, she took me down in my hometown (Charleston) and then she really embarrassed me in Madrid. So I guess I just wanted to show her what New York could do. But man she is a competitor, she is such a fighter. I have so much respect for her. What she's done this year is unfathomable."

Ash had been away from home for six months but managed to maintain consistency. "For me, it's keeping it simple," she said. "It's enjoying my tennis, going out there and playing with freedom. It's being really clear with tactically how I want to play.

Then it just comes down to execution."

It was execution and a determined opponent that cost her making any further progress in the year's final Slam.

What next? Still in the US, Indian Wells in October was on her schedule where there were 1,000 rankings were on offer for the winner. Ash finished the US Open on 10,000 points. The best any challenger could do by winning the US Open was Aryna Sabalenka who would finish on 8,940.

So, not too much to worry about as far as the No. 1 ranking was concerned.

"We'll let this settle and kind of rest a little bit now and take stock a bit," Ash said. "But for us, like we would usually do after every bigger tournament, every kind of phase of the year, I feel like the slams you're kind of building up to it and afterwards there's a reset. For us, it's no different.

"We reset now. We go back, go back to the drawing board, work out what we want to do for the rest of the season."

4

# 2019: A YEAR OF GLORY FOR A NEW STAR WITH NO TICKETS ON HERSELF

Sportsmen call it being "in the zone", a state of heightened proficiency bordering on invincibility. Or, as one dictionary puts it, "you are happy or excited because you are doing something very skilfully and easily".

Ashleigh Barty knows the feeling now.

It's an apt description of how the 23-year-old tennis player took one of the world's most popular and competitive sports by storm in the middle months of 2019, the breakout year that confirmed what people around her have believed since she was a little girl — that she was destined for greatness.

Perfection is one of life's more elusive commodities and nowhere is that truer than in sport. But for 41 glorious days from late May to early July Barty came as close to it as any professional athlete could hope to do.

She was unbeatable for a period during the most important time of the tennis year, winning 15 matches in a row stretching across the French Open, an important grass court event in Birmingham, England, both of which she won, and the biggest challenge of all, Wimbledon.

She rocketed to the top of the rankings, officially becoming the best female player in the world, and then after being temporarily dislodged she did it again and was still at the pinnacle as the end of the year approached. She was not only statistically the best in the business but one of the most popular too.

With the possible exception of cricketer Steve Smith, whose Bradmanesque batting dominated the successful Ashes campaign, no sports star captured the imagination of the Australian public — and the community in general — quite so comprehensively.

That happened for reasons that statistics and scorelines could never adequately explain, or do justice to.

Yes, stellar success had much to do with it — but the way she went about it counted for even more. She played and conducted herself with pride, grace and panache, humility and modesty. She developed an original form of homegrown charisma that was not borrowed from anybody else.

To employ an old Aussie expression, she had no tickets on herself. She made it abundantly clear that winning tennis matches was less important than being a person her family and friends — and anybody else who tuned in to her captivating story — could be proud of.

She is a throwback to the golden era of Australian tennis in the '60s and '70s when old-timers such as Frank Sedgman and his protégé Margaret Court, Rod Laver, John Newcombe and others — not everyone, admittedly, but most of the stars of the era — made it a priority to protect and enhance their own and their country's reputation and image on the world stage.

It may not be entirely coincidental that Laver, the greatest of them all, emerged from the same laid-back Queensland environment as Barty has and that they have so much in common.

**"She gives 100 per cent but doesn't live or die on the outcome..."**

It is probably fair to suggest that even though she is still in her early twenties and with a decade in the spotlight still to come, it is highly likely that Barty will end up being held in much the same esteem as any of the great Australian tennis players of the past, regardless of how her career statistics end up reading.

As it unfolds, her story is becoming so much more than that. All of which is why the applause reached a crescendo off the playing arena in October when the Sport Australia Hall of Fame — a group of more than 500 of the highest achievers across all sports — presented her with its most prestigious and coveted accolade, the Don Award.

The Don is much more than a high-performance award —

it acknowledges qualities such as inspiration, sportsmanship, dignity, humility and courage, as defined by Sir Donald Bradman, the immortal cricketer after whom it is named.

The criteria fits Barty like a glove — and vice versa.

The chairman of the award's selection committee, marathon champion and former director of the Australian Institute of Sport, Rob de Castella, said that what most impressed him was Barty's attitude. "She gives 100 per cent but doesn't live or die on the outcome," he said. "She has a really mature and sensible approach to her career. Whenever there was a setback, there was no woe-is-me, just, 'well, I've got this far, I'll keep persevering'. There is a robustness in her character and a degree of humility that is balanced by her confidence and self-belief. She got to No.1 in the world but in her eyes that didn't necessarily make her better than anyone else. I want the Don award to reflect beyond the scoreboard and to sometimes demonstrate that while it's great to be victorious the way you handle defeat gives a much greater insight into the character of an athlete. In both victory and defeat, Ashleigh has been superb."

The longer the year went, the more the accolades flowed in. In the week before the Hall of Fame presentation the *Financial Review* magazine — seeking to rank the people who wielded the most influence over the social landscape — named her as the "most culturally powerful Australian for 2019", ahead of another indigenous sports star, footballer Adam

Goodes. Two other magazines, *GQ* and *Women's Health*, shortlisted her for their own athlete of the year awards, the first being for both genders and the second for women only. As well, *Google* reported that she was now the most researched Australian of the year.

Her progression from emerging star to within touching distance of greatness was timed to... well, perfection, because it coincided or caught up with national debates and campaigns about a range of social issues, including gender equality, racism, cheating, free speech, religious conviction, homophobia, drug use, gambling excess, and the fine line separating uninhibited personal expression and offensive behaviour.

Much of this was being played out in a sporting context, featuring high-profile footballers, cricketers, tennis players and others, but it wasn't limited to the playing fields, dressing rooms, administrative offices and grandstands.

The community in general became concerned, quite rightly, with the national image when the Test cricket team descended into disgrace for cynically trashing the spirit of that noble old game as well as the rules; when rugby star Israel Folau threatened homosexuals and other sinners with the wrath of Hell; when tennis players Nick Kyrgios and Bernard Tomic defiled their own towering talents and the sport itself with boorish attitudes and behaviour; when a new spotlight was trained on how footy star Adam Goodes had been jeered in a manner widely considered to be the manifestation of an ugly racist underbelly; or when female footballers were mocked on social media for reasons that sometimes had little to do with their ability to play the game.

All of these issues were either still in play or back on the agenda when Barty's big year began.

All of them, and more, transcended sport — to a greater or lesser extent, they were major news stories on every level, of more interest to many people than the re-election of the government, the uncertain economy, climate change or the escalating road toll.

That's because, for better or for worse, Australians have always considered sport to be a KPI — a key performance indicator — when it comes to assessing their place in the world, and the pride they take in it. They are constantly in the market for a hero — someone to identify with proudly.

Despite her relative youth, this has never been lost on Barty. After winning her first round match at the Australian Open as her destiny began to come into sharp focus, an American journalist said to her: "I am going to ask you a foreigner's question. As someone coming here and looking, reading your newspapers, watching your television, there's such a hunger for a champion. Where do you think that comes from? You have a deep, rich tradition in tennis. How does that affect you?"

Barty replied: "I think Australians in general love their sport. That's certainly no secret. We've been very spoiled across all codes and forms of the game to have legends, those that have achieved unthinkable things, especially in tennis. We've had legends throughout all of tennis history in Australia.

"Australians are hungry for sport. They love it. They're addicted to it. I think at this time of the year it always floats around with tennis that they're looking for an Australian player, in particular, to go deep and have a really good run. I try to enjoy it, embrace it and play with freedom."

Against this backdrop, Barty has proven to be precisely the right person in the right place at the right time.

Just when the nation needed a feel-good figure of inspiration carrying no baggage, she arrived with such upbeat impact that it was impossible not to notice.

As a female athlete with an indigenous background, she has not been exempt from the challenges.

She was not born into any special privilege, except for her God-given gift, and has been handed nothing on a silver service, so there has been no reason whatsoever for the public admiration of what she has achieved, and how she has earned it, to be diluted or disrespected, in the way that Kyrgios and Tomic have brought upon themselves.

Those two unfortunate under-achievers weren't born into particularly rarefied air either, which is one of the few things they have in common with Barty. Another is immense, innate talent. And that's about where it stops. Those two difficult dudes haven't worked remotely as hard as she has to make the most of their in-built advantage, and predictably they have not reached anywhere near the heights of achievement that she has.

Indeed, for every positive headline Barty generated during the northern summer there was yet another embarrassing episode in Kyrgios's sad serial, culminating in the men's tour opening two concurrent investigations into his baroque behaviour. Charged with "aggravated behaviour", which covered a number of offences, he was put on probation for six months, fined $37,000 and told to behave himself or spend half a year on the sidelines. He then said he wouldn't be playing for the rest of the year anyway because of a collarbone injury.

For most Australian sports fans, it wasn't just sad to watch, it was infuriating — although many had just stopped caring, unwilling to invest any emotional energy into what was widely perceived as a national embarrassment.

The contrast with Barty is a neatly-packaged, easily observable lesson in life for young people aspiring to anything.

For her, the rewards — both materially and emotionally — have been immense and there is no reason to believe they will not continue to be for as long as she wants that to be the case.

Everything points to a long and successful career ahead.

Many lesser performers on the tennis circuit would be happy to boast an entire career CV containing the high points that 2019 alone has brought her, and it's probably fair to suggest that Barty herself would have thought no differently during a difficult formative period as she wondered whether she was really cut out for a life in professional sport.

## 5

# WHY EVEN THE DOGS ARE BARKING FOR HER

From the moment she arrived at the Australian Open in January, ranked 15, and having been runner-up in the Sydney international prelude event the previous week for the second year in a row, the scriptwriters barely paused for breath.

In Melbourne, she reached the quarter-finals of a Grand Slam event for the first time, easily outstripping her best performance at her "home" major since she first played it as a 15-year-old in 2012, losing in the first round.

After reaching the third round in 2017 and 2018, this time she went two better, beating former world No.1 Maria Sharapova along the way, before going down 6-4 6-1 to the Czech Republic's Petra Kvitova. She was the first Australian to make the quarters at Melbourne Park since the talented but troubled Jelena Dokic in 2009.

Next came the Fed Cup — the women's equivalent of the Davis Cup, which Australia had won seven times but not since 1974. They weren't expected to change that this time, either. That is not until Barty went into action in the first round in the American city of Asheville, defeating the USA's Sofia Kenin and Madison Keys in straight sets and teaming with 20-year-old Priscilla Hon to take out Danielle Collins and Nicola Melicher in two in the doubles. Then, against a formidable Belarus in the semi-final in Brisbane in April she accounted for Victoria Azarenka and Aryna Sabalenka without dropping a set and then partnered Sam Stosur to a three-set decider over the same two girls, setting up a final against France in Perth in November.

"She takes great delight in representing Australia at this level"

This was no ordinary win, and not simply because of the long drought her country had experienced in this competition, having not contested a final since three years before she was born and not won one for more than three decades.

That certainly hasn't been her fault. She takes great delight in representing Australia at this level and it shows on the scoreboard, with a 10-1 record in singles and 7-1 in doubles, and she is the first player ever to play and win every possible match on the way to the final.

That's why in June she was the proud recipient — and the first from Australia — of the International Tennis Federation's Fed Cup Heart Award, which recognises players who have represented their country with distinction, shown exceptional courage on court and demonstrated outstanding commitment to their team.

Her Fed Cup record revives memories of two of Australia's all-time great players in team tennis, one from long ago in Frank Sedgman and another much more recently, Lleyton Hewitt.

In the Davis Cup, Sedgman won 16 of 19 singles matches and was undefeated in nine doubles encounters from 1949 until 1952 and played in three winning finals. Hewitt, playing much more often than Sedgman did in the old Challenge Round system, won a record 59 matches — 42 singles and 17 doubles — while losing only 14 singles and seven doubles from 1999 until recently.

Barty's Heart Award came with a cheque for $14,426 for the charity of her choice, which the owner of four dogs — Rudy, Maxi, Affie and Chino, a "mixture of fluff-ball breeds" — promptly gave to the RSPCA, for which she is an ambassador.

Her love for dogs — all animals, in fact — is one of the reasons her personality attracts such empathy. "What's better than a tough day on the court? Coming home and giving them a cuddle on the couch is one of the most simple but enjoyable things for me to do, win or lose they love me exactly the same," she says.

"Seeing anyone mistreat animals is very hard to bear."

Aside from the Fed Cup, after the Open her busy tournament schedule took her to America, firstly Indian Wells where she reached the third round and then to Miami, where she went all the way for the fourth Women's Tennis Association tournament win of her career, adding it to the 2017 Malaysian Open, and the Nottingham Open and the Elite Trophy in Zhuhai, China, both in 2018.

The prestigious Miami Open was a major stepping stone, a flashing neon light illuminating the way ahead. It is no run-of-the mill whistle-stop. Established in 1985, it and Indian Wells enjoy pretty much equal billing as the second most important events in America behind the US Open, with more than $10m in prizemoney, with 96 men and 96 women — not the usual 64 — playing for 12 days, not just a week, with the winners taking home more than one million dollars.

It wasn't just a big pay-day for Barty, it was a confidence booster because she beat three top 10 players, including No.2 Kvitova in the quarter-finals and No.7 Karolina Pliskova in the final.

Having started the year ranked 15, she now found herself in the top 10 for the first time.

Her campaign was gathering serious pace — next stop Europe, and the clay courts that have never really been her go. Not yet.

In preparation for the French Open, she played only two events on the dusty red dirt. In Madrid, she got to the quarters before being derailed by world No.3 Simone Halep of Romania, followed by a second round loss to France's Kristina

Mladenovic in Rome, which at the time she struggled slightly to deal with. "It was the only match of the whole year (to date) that I walked off the court and was a little bit disappointed with how I played and how I was out there." The negative emotions didn't last long — with Barty they very seldom do.

6

# OPPORTUNITY COMES CALLING... IN FRENCH

In most elite sporting careers there comes a moment of opportunity, of beckoning destiny, when the gods of greatness roll out the red carpet and invite you to walk it — if you can, if you want it enough, if you're not afraid to ask yourself a few hard questions and to trust the answers you supply.

Sometimes it is recognisable in advance and sometimes it is not. Sometimes it is planned with perfect precision and sometimes it seems almost accidental.

It is seldom straightforward, often unpredictable. Luck can occasionally be almost as important as talent, work ethic, confidence and preparation.

So nobody knew for sure quite what to expect when Barty arrived in the city of love, Paris, for the French Open in early June. She had ample good form behind her, resulting in a career-best ranking of eight, more peace of mind and self-belief than at any previous stage of her career, better fitness levels, an improved serve, a support team that was providing nothing but positive vibes, and a disinclination to fret over two salient facts

— that she had been to the fourth round of a major tournament only once in 17 attempts, and she was not as comfortable on clay courts as she was on hardcourts and grass.

Seeded according to her ranking, she was, theoretically, expected to make the quarter-finals, and nobody — with the possible exception of herself — would regard it as an under-achievement if she did that and no more.

But before a ball was struck in anger, it was impossible for anyone — including her — to know just how loud that knock was. Opportunity was about to bash the door down in a number of unforeseen ways.

The first bit of good luck she — and the other 127 women in the field — had was the withdrawal of her regular foe Kvitova, the No.3 seed, with an arm injury. Then two former world No.1s, Maria Sharapova and Angelique Kerber both lost in the first round.

Barty took full advantage of the comfortable draw provided by her elevated seeding disposing of Americans Jessica Pegula and Danielle Collins and Germany's Andrea Petkovic, all in straight sets, conceding only 16 games in total, or fewer than three per set. This was clinical carnage of the sort often seen in the early rounds of women's tournaments, when the gap between the stars and the also-rans is more obvious than it usually is with the gentlemen. It is not too taxing physically, two sets normally occupying little more than an hour's exertion, and such scorelines are good for morale and confidence just as long as they do not become ego trips, a contingency no more likely to bring Barty undone than the earth opening up and swallowing her.

But as she paused to take stock after three rounds — almost the halfway point — you wouldn't have blamed her if she had offered a small smile to the skies. That's because the third round had also proven to be the burial ground for three of her most dangerous rivals, the reigning No.1, Japan's Naomi Osaka, the legendary American Serena Williams and another former No.1, the Czech Republic's Karolina Pliskova.

That still left world No.3 and defending champion Simona Halep in her path if she could dispose of Americans Sofia Kenin, 20, and Madison Keys, 24, the 14th seed, to get that far, which she did, dropping one set to Kenin and none to Keys.

But, hey presto — the Gods had smiled again. An almost unknown American teenager, Amanda Ansimova, 17, had eliminated Halep and given herself a shot at unlikely glory. She made a statement to the effect that her big win was no fluke when she took the first set off Barty in a tie-breaker in the semi-final, but then succumbed bravely in the remaining two stanzas.

That left Barty up against another Czech, 20-year-old Marketa Vondrousova, in the decider, in which she was never troubled to prevail with the loss of just one game in the first set and three in the second. Basically, it was a no-contest.

For both men and women, the big four tennis tournaments are never handed to anyone on a platter. But the luck of the draw can sometimes play a significant part. Barty's towering triumph was well and truly earned in very emphatic fashion, but it is, perhaps, fair to suggest that she enjoyed a rails run, as they say in horse racing.

She was confronted by only one seeded opponent, Keys, who has never been a world-beater, and the other six she had to deal with were all ranked in the 20s, 30s and beyond. Three of her opponents were aged 20 or less, and two of those, Anisimova, 17, and Vondrousova, just short of her 20th birthday, were in the firing line when the stakes were at their highest and the pressure most intense. For Barty, these were very different assignments than, say, the iron-willed Williams would have been — but as they say, all you have to do in any sporting contest is beat whoever you're up against, and she did that to, yes, perfection.

In the context of Australian tennis, it was hugely historic — the breaking of a long drought dating back to shortly after the beginning of the Open era in 1968. That year, American Nancy Richey triumphed at Roland Garros, then Australia's Margaret Court — still the most prolific winner of major tournaments in women's tennis history — won in 1969 and 1970, followed by another Australian, Evonne Goolagong Cawley, in 1971, and Court again in 1973. So the gap to Barty was 46 years. Ken Rosewall and Rod Laver won in 1968 and 1969, the last men to do so.

The victory elevated Barty from No.8 to No.2 in

the rankings, putting her on the brink of another historic accomplishment — no Australian woman had been No.1 since Goolagong for two weeks in April 1976. So there was ample incentive to keep going hard.

The headline-writers love an alliteration or a rhyme so they were almost unanimously happy to label this the "Barty party" — and the phrase instantly began to trend worldwide on Twitter. But it was nothing of the sort. Well, not to the extent that might have been easily forgiven.

**"I know they were living through every single point with me"**

She gathered her team around her, or those who were on hand — oddly, her parents, Rob and Josie had flown from Brisbane to Europe but arrived in London just hours before the French final and had little choice but to sit tight there and watch it on TV.

Their daughter took that in her measured stride too.

"There was no physical possibility they could get to Paris, but I knew they were watching, I know they were living through every single point with me, and every single ride," she said.

"I will see them tomorrow, give them a big hug and a kiss obviously. It will be really nice to see them again because it's been a few weeks."

The "party", she said, would be just a couple of quiet beers and a steak for dinner — she couldn't have made it sound any more Aussie if she'd opted for a pie 'n' sauce and a Vegemite sandwich. She does like Vegemite — and it likes her. Later in the year, the makers of the famous breakfast spread — which she always carries with her overseas — renamed it Bartymite in her honour for a month. Accolades don't come much more Australian than that.

She could, of course, have afforded to splurge on the finest French fizz and classic cuisine in any of the upmarket dining establishments that are so much a part of Parisian life, having just pocketed a cheque for a tournament record $US2.62m, taking her career earnings at that point to past $US10m, more than half of it in the first half of 2019. But it had always been, and remains, a rare day when Barty is ever heard talking about money. Most certainly, she does not have much, if anything, in common with her boorish compatriot Tomic, who has been known to sneer at his critics that he spends his time counting his millions — and they don't.

Indeed, it was later reported that she had less than $1000 in her investment platform when she took a break from the sport. Her father closed Barty Investments Pty Ltd in May 2014, but when she returned in 2016 it was re-registered to protect her earnings from prizemoney, as well as endorsements from which she earns about $400,000 a year, according to the *Herald Sun* newspaper.

Successful athletes often talk about "living the dream", seeing their childhood fantasies materialise, and the Parisian epiphany was the moment that became tangible for Barty — even though she said: "This is just incredible, I never dreamt that I'd be sitting here with this trophy at the French Open. I mean, obviously, we have dreams and goals as children, but this is incredible.

**"I never dreamt that I'd be sitting here with this trophy at the French Open"**

"It's been an incredible couple of weeks, that's for sure. I think any time I can play my brand of tennis, I know that I can match against the best in the world. For the last fortnight, the stars have aligned for me. I have been able to play really good tennis when I have needed it."

Not for the first time — and certainly not for the last — she paid tribute to the team around her, particularly her previously little-known coach Craig Tyzzer, her childhood mentor, Jim Joyce, and performance guru Ben Crowe, a former Nike director who worked with seven-time world champion surfer Stephanie Gilmore and former tennis superstar Andre Agassi as well as cricketers and footballers.

"This is a celebration of not just the last two or three weeks but the last two or three years for myself and my team.

I have an extraordinary group of genuine, authentic people around me. This is just a by-product of what we've been able to do, all the work we have done, and I'm speechless," she said.

She might have been lost for words — well, she wasn't really, because her victory media conference was lengthy, wide-ranging, articulate, emotional and informative — but back in Australia, nobody else was.

Suddenly, talk-back radio, the letters pages in newspapers and all forms of social media were overflowing with comments about her. And the remarkable aspect of that was that it was impossible to stumble across a single negative one. That is most unusual. Lofty achievement of any description usually attracts a few narks and trolls just wanting to stand out in the crowd and hear the sound of their own voices, but with this new phenomenon it seemed there was simply nothing to criticise.

People — and not just tennis buffs or sports fans in general, but the wider public — rapidly realised that here was a new shining light on centre stage who was iron-willed and fiercely-focussed and yet in everything she did, the definition of classy.

In short, she was making Australia proud.

And really, she was just getting started. There was more to come — immediately. Much more.

# 7

# FRIEND AND FOE ON TOP OF THE WORLD

Barty departed Paris for the short trip across the English Channel to decidedly less glamourous Birmingham for a Premier level grass court tournament which is regarded as a Wimbledon warm-up in much the same way the Queen's Club championship in London is for the men. Barty had almost won it two years earlier, when beaten in the final by Kvitova. This time, the stakes were significantly higher. If she could go one better and become the first Australian to win it, providing the incumbent No.1 Osaka bowed out early — which she did in the second round — Barty would become the new queen of the sport.

Technically, if you're No.1 you're entitled to be regarded as the best player in the world, although it's not always as simple as that. The rankings sometimes work — like God — in mysterious ways, such as when Denmark's Caroline Wozniacki finished 2010 and 2011 at No.1 without winning a major tournament in either year, in fact not until she claimed the Australian Open seven years later.

Serena Williams has been ranked No.1 on six different occasions between 2002 and 2017 for a total of 319 weeks, which makes her indisputably the best women's player during that period, and in the eyes of most she probably still is, even though motherhood has meant that she has spent two years well short of the official top rung. And when Canadian teenager Biance Andreescu toppled her in the US Open final, it gave the new champion an 8-0 record over top 10 players for the year, which some might consider entitled her to be the best even if it did mean she was ranked only fifth.

All of that said, whoever is No.1 is fully entitled to soak up the applause and the pride which comes with such an important achievement, and Barty would certainly be no exception.

To do it, she would have to adjust from the Continental clay of the previous month to the grass — but that wasn't a problem. She has always liked the green stuff — and not necessarily on tennis courts either. As part of her preparation she relaxed with a couple of games of golf, out of public sight and mind.

"Changing surfaces is kind of a new start," she said later, speaking to the Women's Tennis Association Insider website. "It was coming in fresh and a little bit of the element of the unknown. This is always a time of the year that I love to play. I knew it wasn't going to be perfect tennis and I just had to try and get my feet stuck into the tournament and get my feet used to the surface as quickly as possible. But it's a surface that I love to play on and always brings a smile on that first practice session on grass."

So speaks a throwback to the original glory days of Australian tennis when the French Open was the only one of the four majors not played on grass, and the Down Under stars of both genders thrived on it, especially at Wimbledon and, of course, at home.

Here, Barty may have again breathed a little easier when Kvitova withdrew with an arm injury. But she was quickly into confident stride, taking out Donna Vekic, Jennifer Brady, Venus Williams and Barbora Strycova without dropping a set, bringing her up against her new doubles partner and close friend Julia Goerges of Germany in the final, with much more than the prizemoney of about $1.6m riding on it.

Both began their Birmingham campaigns by teaming together for two matches before both withdrew to fry bigger fish.

It was Barty who caught the whopper, winning 6-3, 7-5 in a tight fight, her 12th victory in a row. Occasionally these events, where so much is at stake, are dog eat dog, no beg pardons, may the Devil take the hindmost as the late Kerry Packer used to say — but this wasn't one of them. It was exactly the opposite.

When they came together at the net, they publicly congratulated each other in warm terms. "She almost made me cry," Barty said. "She's just an incredible human being. There's probably only a handful of other people I'd like to share that moment with."

Goerges, seven years Barty's senior, is a good player who has

> **"She almost made me cry, she's just an incredible human being."**

been ranked as high as nine, with five titles to her name and an appearance in the semi-finals at Wimbledon the previous year.

Although they had only recently started teaming together, the pair are old mates. "Jules has always made time for me ever since I started on tour, we have always enjoyed practising together and spending time with each other. It's hard playing a friend in a final but in a final I think you'd love to play a friend knowing you have both earned that spot.

"Jules and I are very close and it's tough whenever you are playing a friend, but I know that I respect her and she respects me enough to put that aside when we're on the court. As soon as we shake hands no matter who has won or lost the relationship doesn't change and it's a testament to Jules as a character."

It made her the 27th woman to ascend to the top spot since the women's rankings were introduced in 1975 — two years after the men — and only the fifth Australian of either gender. Apart from Cawley's brief reign, John Newcombe was on top of the men's rankings for eight weeks in 1974, Pat Rafter for one week in 1999 and Lleyton Hewitt for an impressive 80 weeks from November 2001.

Barty's response was to channel Prime Minister Scott

Morrison's jubilant "how good is Australia?!" catchphrase after his election win a few weeks earlier.

"There you go. How bloody good!" she said.

"It's been a goal of mine, that's no secret. And it's amazing what happens when you put your hopes and dreams out into the universe and do the work. It's amazing."

Astonishingly, it had been only three years since Barty had returned to the game in early 2016 after a mind-clearing sabbatical of more than a year with a ranking of 623, meaning she didn't just have a mountain to climb — she was starting at sea-level with the summit of Mount Everest looming above.

Her arrival represents one of the most — to employ one of her own favourite words — "incredible" comebacks in all sporting history. In fact, her fellow Queenslander, sports columnist Robert Craddock, declared it the most impressive Australian sports story of the 21st century.

And it was acknowledged as such by many of her rivals on the circuit, who were quick to message her with not just their congratulations but recognition that it was no fluke, but had been well and truly earned.

Prominent among them was American Chris Evert, the WTA's first No.1 when she took top spot in 1975 and held it for an initial stint of 26 weeks. As of 2018, a newly-minted trophy named after her is presented to the winner, firstly Simona Halep and now Barty. It features a silver "star map" tennis ball with thousands of tiny dots representing female professionals from the past and into the future. All No.1s are marked with a diamond.

Evert, who retired in 1989 with 18 Grand Slam titles, wrote on Twitter: "A big congratulations to @ashbar76. Tremendous story, talent, and most importantly, person."

Asked if she could have envisaged this lofty status when her comeback began, Barty smiled and said: "We had a very vague plan to try and get back obviously into the rhythm of it and to be playing again. But certainly not for it to happen this quickly. It's always a goal to try to be the best. It's ultimately why we train, why we compete and play, but for it to happen in this way is amazing."

And again she deflected the credit to her team, "who have put so much time and invested so much passion and energy into my career and try to make me the best I can be". This had become a mantra, a recurring theme, and there was very good for reason for it.

8

# A TARGET TO TOY WITH: TO INFINITY AND BEYOND

So far so... well, not merely so good. So terrific. Two titles and 12 wins and counting in the space of 27 days. How far can this whip-cracking winning streak take her? The answer was not immediately forthcoming because a recurring minor elbow strain prompted Barty and her handlers to scratch from the Eastbourne tournament in the south of England, traditionally the curtain-raiser for Wimbledon and an event that had played a major role in her comeback three years earlier.

For most tennis players the manicured lawns of London SW19 are the sport's spiritual home. They might not necessarily enjoy playing on the one surface they rarely encounter for the rest of the year but even the born and bred clay courters acknowledge it as the Holy Grail, an irresistible challenge. For Barty, it means a little more than most.

For it was here that she first really put her name up in lights, winning the girls singles title at the age of 15 in 2011 and reaching a junior world ranking of No.2. Now, eight years later, she was back in very different circumstances, the first

Australian to be seeded first since Cawley was in her prime, and given her red-hot form and proficiency on grass, the warm favourite to take out the title.

This was to be Barty's fourth appearance in the singles draw, the first two, in 2012 and 2017, seeing her despatched in the first round, while she won two matches in 2018. So she was accustomed to flying under the radar, undistracted by public or media attention — but that wasn't going to be easy to achieve this time. "I like to keep things as low-key as much as possible," she said. "But the last month, the last two weeks have been a bit of a whirlwind." Still, London is a big city and she was able to travel around on the Underground without being recognised, and even kept in the background when she visited the home of cricket, Lord's, to watch the Australian men's team play England in the World Cup — at least until she was ushered into the inner sanctum to meet the captain Aaron Finch and his troops for a photo shoot.

Barty, from suburban Ipswich in Queensland, and Finch, from country Colac in Victoria, hit it off immediately — he was more thrilled than she was, his wife said — because they have a lot in common, both having worked diligently to prove to themselves and others that they are good enough to make it to the top.

When the iconic tournament began, she sounded cool, calm and confident. Interviewed on TV by well-known Australian coach Darren Cahill before the first match against China's Zheng

Saisai, she said the only thing that had changed was that her self-belief — never all that fragile anyway — had been reinforced and when asked if she could win back to back majors she grinned and said, "Why not?!"

Even the organisers seemed unsure just where she stood in terms of public profile, and so did one important section of the Australian media, the Seven TV Network. She and Zheng were consigned to the relative backwater of Court Two with the match beginning while an all-Australian men's match between Nick Kyrgios and Jordon Thompson was progressing to the full five sets before Kyrgios prevailed in his customary colourful, unpredictable fashion.

Seven elected to show it all with only intermittent updates of Barty's straight-sets win, leaving the full coverage to Foxtel's paying customers, which infuriated those fans at home who could not understand why the intensely annoying Kyrgios would take precedence over the far more likeable and successful Barty. Clearly discomfited by the barrage of criticism, Seven claimed that the men's match was a much closer contest than Barty's "one-sided" opener, in which she dropped only six games. The social media verdict: It's a joke!

Two days later, the schedulers — deliberately or not, who knows? — avoided a repeat by starting Barty's match against Belgium's Alison Van Uytvanck well before Kyrgios was due to take on Spanish superstar Rafael Nadal. Barty took less than an hour to prevail again dropping only four games and was back in the dressing room long before Nadal set about formalising his thinly-veiled contempt for Kyrgios, who had — as only he would — prepared for the centre court encounter with a big night at the Dog & Fox pub just up the road from the courts.

Barty's status was finally ticked off by the schedulers in round three when she was assigned centre court, although that might not have been entirely unrelated to the identity of her opponent, Harriet Dart, 22, who is English. Wimbledon always loves to look after its own, which is entirely reasonable — so does the Australian Open. "I won't be playing a British crowd, I'll be playing against Harriet," Barty said when asked if she expected to be the villain for once. "Yes, she'll get more support, being in Britain, as I would if we were in Australia."

**"I promised myself I would smile and try to take it all in"**

And so she did — to very little avail. Ranked 182 and needing a wildcard to get into the draw, the inexperienced Dart was swept aside 6-1 6-1 in just 53 minutes by Barty's formidable all-round game, every aspect of which was so in tune that one commentator was prompted to describe it as "painting with all the colours".

It was the best moment of the tournament so far for Barty because of the exhilarating experience of being on such hallowed ground. "It was a very special moment walking onto centre court — I promised myself I would smile and try to take it all in," she said.

That turned out to be an astute thing to do because you never know with these things when — or if — your next opportunity will come along.

She was back out on court two for round four against American Alison Riske, which prompted another minor controversy when it was suggested in some quarters that she should have been on centre court again, possibly at the expense of Nadal, who was a virtual fixture there.

The Spaniard was unimpressed, replying: "I am the No.2 and I won 18 Grand Slams. My feeling is today I am little bit more than Ashleigh Barty."

It was a perfectly acceptable response, a reminder that for all her new-found status Barty was still a newcomer to the tennis stratosphere — and he certainly got no argument from her. "I'll play on any court to which I am scheduled," she said.

Riske was a 29-year-old American with a grass court record impressive enough to suggest that after three virtual walkovers, Barty was in for a significantly more challenging assignment this time.

Win this and she would be through to the quarter-finals where, almost certainly, the most formidable figure in the history of women's tennis, Serena Williams, would be waiting. This loomed as the most magnetic women's match-up of the first week, if not the entire tournament — the old matriarch versus the new queen.

Even Williams made little attempt to disguise her anticipation of it, even though she had another match to play and win before it would happen. "I've been watching her closely," she said.

The prospect of the two meeting had been made all the more interesting when Williams, in an interview before the tournament started, spoke about Barty's ascension to the throne in a way that some observers found to be slightly patronising, especially when she appeared to be unaware that the Australian was, in fact, now No.1. Few would give much credence to her not knowing that so it smacked of mind games.

Former Australian circuit player Sam Groth savaged her in a syndicated newspaper column, saying she was guilty of disrespect. Williams, who possibly would have little knowledge of who the modestly accomplished but well-informed Groth is, let alone much time for his opinions, retorted that she had no idea what he was talking about, and that she, along with everybody else in the locker room, was a Barty admirer.

Barty, as usual, was unfazed.

As the potential showdown drew nearer, she had no interest in talking about playing Williams, saying — astutely and presciently — "I'll give the athlete's answer to that, 'I'm just going to worry about Alison first'."

Riske was never likely to be a soft touch — she is the

daughter of a Secret Service operative who guarded several Presidents before retiring when she was three years old so he could make her his priority.

So when Barty opened proceedings with an astonishing four aces in the first game and went on to claim the set 6-3, nobody was taking anything for granted on either side of the net.

That was as good as it got against the fiercely competitive American, who took control as Barty's serve deserted her — she was landing her first delivery at only 55 per cent. Barty became increasingly tentative as the confidence levels of both women crossed paths like two elevators going up and down.

Implementing advice from an expert analyst, Craig O'Shannessy, who is Australian, Riske targeted Barty's forehand and levelled the match 6-2 in the second, then stormed home, 6-3, for possibly the best win of her career.

Australia, all of it, groaned in dismay. But Barty didn't.

Her response, delivered to the media, provided yet more proof that she was a class act in every respect.

"Absolutely no regrets," she said. "We've planned our days and prepared the best we can. Today wasn't my day. I didn't win a tennis match. It's not the end of the world. It's a game. I love playing the game. I do everything in my power to try to win every single tennis match, but that's not the case. It's disappointing right now. Give me an hour or so, we'll be all good. The sun's still going to come up tomorrow."

## "It's disappointing right now. The sun's still going to come up tomorrow"

Reflecting on her stunning streak, she added: "Overall, it's been a hell of a trip. Disappointed right now, obviously it's a tough pill to swallow. In the same breath, it's been an incredible few months.

"New ground for me here at Wimbledon. This is the best we've done. Also proud of the fact what we've been able to do over the last eight weeks. The consistency we've brought day in and day out, has been next to none (sic). That's one of the best things about this trip.

"There are so many things we wish we had done, the what-ifs. That's not what we try to focus on. We focus on the positives. The last two months, last six months, and for this year, it's been incredible.

"Today wasn't my day but that's not going to define us as a team, it's not going to define me as a person. That's the most important thing."

There was, perhaps, only one thing missing from her dialogue with the international sportswriters.

After her first win, against Zheng, she had told them: "We kind of came into it thinking like Hakuna Matata." Her inquisitors recognised that as a reference to the "no worries" philosophy of the star of the Disney animated musical *The Lion King*, but thought nothing more of it.

Then, after the Van Uytvanck match, she said: "I chat to my niece over and over and she just tells me, 'you can go to infinity and beyond'." That's a line from another popular Disney film, *Toy Story*. Again, it passed without comment.

Saddling up again following the Dart demolition, she went with: "I think for me sometimes I look at a shot, play a shot, and I think the sea is always greener in someone else's lake."

Finally, back home in Australia, the Sunday morning sports show on ABC TV, *Offsiders*, twigged. That one was also a Disney creation, from *The Little Mermaid*.

Barty, it seemed, had been amusing herself with a little game at the media's expense. In fact, though, like most things she does, it wasn't as simple as all that. One of her support team — probably Crowe — had devised the ploy as a way of lightening the mood of the press conferences, which some players, especially young ones, sometimes find intimidating and stressful.

The celebrated Australian football coach David Parkin used to refer to the after-match interrogation as "the fifth quarter" and often said it could be more difficult than the main task at hand, winning the game.

At Wimbledon, no one needed to look far for an example of this. Naomi Osaka, who Barty deposed as No.1, was beaten in the first round by Kazakhstan's Yulia Putintsova, who had also upset her at the Birmingham tournament a week earlier.

Having refused to attend the media conference the first time, which is against the rules, she turned up this time, provided monosyllabic answers to 10 questions and then, asked if she was struggling to adjust to fame, the 21-year-old Japanese prodigy asked for permission to leave "because I feel like I'm going to cry". This was difficult to watch because Osaka is a pleasant and popular personality who never invites negative responses to her behaviour in any way, but who was just distraught after a tough day at the office.

Yes, disappointment can be hard to handle on the big stage. Which just makes Barty's poise and aplomb all the more impressive.

# 9

# UNMISTAKEABLY FROM THE LAND DOWN UNDER

With three of the four major tournaments behind her and the fourth one, the US Open, only two months ahead, it was time for the new queen to pause for breath and reflect on what had been achieved and what was still to come. Ditto for her fans, which by now included most people in Australia with any interest in sport — and that's the vast majority of the population of 25 million. There was never any doubt about where and how she would choose to recharge the batteries — she travelled straight back to Ipswich — an urban region of 200,000 people southeast of the Brisbane metropolitan area — to reconnect with family and friends, where the hero's welcome was low-key because, well, that's the way she likes it.

There are multiple reasons for her popularity at home and by no means are they all to do with her ability to wield a tennis racquet. One of the main ones is that she is, simply, so very Australian.

This isn't about how she looks or how she speaks, neither of which are particularly distinctive, it's just the package she presents — a knockabout personality totally devoid of posturing or big-noting, not the slightest element of drama queen, a love not just of tennis but all sports (a very Australian characteristic) and even an apparent disdain for a champagne lifestyle when a couple of quiet beers will do.

She gives the distinct impression that she would be more than happy to go to a backyard barbecue at anybody's place and spend the afternoon chewing the fat about the footy or the family.

And of course her indigenous heritage is extremely important — to her personally, and to a nation that continues to struggle to integrate fully with the original Australians, sometimes in sports arenas as much as anywhere else.

Robert Barty, Ashleigh's father, is descended from the Ngarigo people, who originated from southeast NSW from Canberra and the Snowy Mountains down to the Victorian border, while her mother is the daughter of English immigrants.

Barty, whose great-grandmother was a Ngarigo woman, told journalist Konrad Marshall in 2017 that her heritage was "really important to me. I've always had that olive complexion and the squished nose, and I just think it's important to do the best I can to be a good role model".

Naturally, the indigenous community has embraced her enthusiastically. In 2017, she was named Sportswoman of the Year in the National Dreamtime Awards and in 2018 Tennis Australia appointed her National Indigenous Tennis

Ambassador, a role which aims to introduce the sport to more than 1000 children in the Northern Territory.

Until her French Open breakthrough, this aspect of her identity was less widely-known.

Welcometocountry.org, which describes itself as an independent indigenous news/media website that publishes "news often ignored by mainstream media", claimed that there were people who actively tried to obliterate that identity by twice removing references to it from her Wikipedia page.

"Even though removing the word does nothing to change who Barty is, we feel its important to highlight that people are willing to try and deny readers the chance to learn that she is in fact an indigenous woman," the site said. "While these actions may seem petty, they are an attack against indigenous identity."

While racial politics might be simmering in the background, to Barty it appears to be just white noise, so to speak, not something in which she has been inclined to immerse herself.

As a role model, however, she is following in the footsteps of two of the most famous sportswomen Australia has ever produced, sprinter Cathy Freeman, the heroine of the 2000 Sydney Olympics both on and off the track, and — more explicitly, by far — Evonne Goolagong Cawley, the exceptional tennis player of the 1970s and 80s.

Barty has formed a powerful relationship with Cawley, with whom she has so much in common. The young

Goolagong, a Wiradjuri woman whose stupendous talent saw her plucked from the obscurity of the dusty country town of Barellan in NSW as a young teenager and taken to Sydney for coaching and development, went on to forge a career second only to the immortal Margaret Court among Australians.

**"While these actions may seem petty, they are an attack against indigenous identity"**

She won the Australian Open four times in a row between 1974 and 1977, Wimbledon twice in 1971 and, as a mother, in 1980 and the French Open in 1971 as well as making the final of the US Open four times in a row between 1973 and 1976. In all, she made 18 Grand Slam finals, had an overall win-loss record of 704 to 165, which included 86 titles, as well as her brief stint as World No.1.

But there is much more to her reputation than statistics, as hugely impressive as those are.

Cawley's laid-back, pleasant personality and willingness to give back to the game that made her rich and famous puts her well and truly in the conversation when it comes to identifying the most admired and respected performer in the history of women's sport in Australia, up there — at least — with iconic figures such as runners Betty Cuthbert, Raelene Boyle and Cathy Freeman; swimmers Dawn Fraser and Shane Gould; and cyclist Anna Meares, among others.

While it is too early to place Barty in that rarefied company just yet, it is where she may well be heading.

Cawley is her mentor and her hero and she makes no secret of it.

When Barty was burnt out to the point where she needed to take a sabbatical from tennis in 2014, Cawley was quick to offer some very culture-specific advice: "Go and wet a line!" — go fishing, in other words.

When she became the first Australian since Cawley to win in Paris, and then followed her into the No.1 ranking, Barty acknowledged the help Cawley had provided, as well as the inspiration she had been to generations of Aboriginal kids, helping forge a path for indigenous tennis. Barty was just one more beneficiary of this.

For her part, Cawley couldn't have been more pleased or generous in her congratulations.

"Ash is a very worthy number one and winning at the French will have given her even more confidence," she said in a statement to the media. "I am so proud that another Aboriginal player sits on top of the rankings in women's tennis, particularly a young lady who conveys such happiness in all she does.

"She really enjoys being out there and she has become an

outstanding and inspirational example to all Australians. Well done Ash — long may your success continue."

Typically, Barty was quick to deflect the praise, saying she had a long way to go to be considered worthy of comparison. "I'm nowhere near her status," Barty said. "To be mentioned in the same sentence is incredible. Evonne, she's an amazing human being and has set the tone for so many Australians and so many indigenous Australians around our country and around the world.

"What she has done in her career was incredible and what she continues to do off the court for us as a sport is amazing."

There is no particular link with Freeman but there are some similarities, both having grown up in Queensland, and both having doubted themselves as they set out, wide-eyed and ambitious, to conquer the world. Freeman came of age on a much bigger stage but Barty's is plenty big enough, especially when the backdrop is Wimbledon or the Australian Open.

10

# WHY IT'S LADIES FIRST FOR ASH AND THE GIRLS

Barty's arrival as an authentic global star was well-timed for another important reason. She has caught perhaps the most powerful wave in Australian sport for at least the past five years — a tsunami, in fact. This has been the rise and rise of women's sport across diverse disciplines, ranging from all the football codes — especially AFL and soccer — through cricket, horse racing, surfing, cycling, golf and even boxing, as well as the more traditional distaff pursuits such as netball, swimming, athletics, basketball and, yes, tennis.

Professionalism and media attention — and therefore public interest — has increased in leaps and bounds, which has been collectively and mutually beneficial in many important ways. While the various sports are in competition with each other for talent, funding and exposure, whenever one team or individual achieves something impressive it enhances the proposition that women's sport in general is becoming more and more attractive to sponsors, spectators and other influencers. They bounce off each other and take turns in leading the way forward in what is still a work very much in progress.

So there was a certain serendipity when Barty won in Birmingham, claiming the No.1 ranking, on the same day as prominent surfer Sally Fitzgibbons won the World Surf League's Rio pro event and also climbed to No.1 in the rankings, while hitherto little-known golfer Hannah Green won the women's PGA championship in Minneapolis by a single shot, meaning her first international victory was in a major tournament.

Barty is a golfer herself and takes a close interest in surfing through seven-times world champion Stephanie Gilmore, who is one of her best friends. With surfing joining tennis as an Olympic sport in Tokyo 2020 she and Gilmore — and Fitzgibbons — could end up team-mates under the five rings.

It added up to a red-letter day not just for Barty, Green and Fitzgibbons themselves but for administrators working hard to maximise the opportunities available to girls.

The trio shared the front page of the nation's biggest-selling newspaper, the *Herald Sun*, under the headline "Our Wonder Women".

"The past 24 hours will no doubt have lasting impact on inspiring future generations of young girls wanting to take up sport and from those many, perhaps a few will become world champions too," said Kate Palmer, chief executive of Sport Australia, the Federal Government body responsible for promoting and funding sport.

Pointing out that Barty had been inspired by Cawley and that

Green had once benefited from a scholarship bearing the name of Australia's best-ever female golfer, Karrie Webb, Palmer added: "These examples show the enduring value of sport's role models."

Victorian Institute of Sport chief Anne Marie Harrison said: "There is no doubt this kind of success has a knock-on effect for young people, girls particularly.

"These have been wins from humble champions who take nothing for granted and show gratitude."

Barty is famously multi-talented at sport and could have chosen any one of several others in which to specialise. As has been widely documented, she dropped out of tennis for a while to play cricket semi-professionally and is also a competent and enthusiastic golfer, a sport in which her father was accomplished and in which her boyfriend, Gary Kissick, is making a mark of his own as trainee PGA professional at the Brookwater Golf and Country Club.

She is a fanatical fan of the Richmond Tigers, one of the oldest and most powerful AFL clubs in Australia, now 2019 Premiers for the second time in three years. She is close friends with the team's captain, Trent Cotchin, a winner of the Brownlow medal for the best player in the competition. When the Tigers gathered in fancy dress to celebrate on the Monday after their latest triumph, Cotchin arrived carrying a tennis racquet and dressed as Barty. On tour, she always has a footy with her and kicks it around to warm up for matches.

Growing up, she also played netball but decided to focus

on tennis because she thought netball was "a girl's game" and because her two older sisters, Sara and Ali, were better at it than she was. The flirtation with cricket came about when, after the US Open in 2014, she decided to take a break from tennis because she wasn't enjoying it as much as she should have been — in fact, she had become thoroughly disillusioned with the demanding lifestyle — and wanted to see what else life had on offer for a while.

At the time she was ranked outside the top 200 in singles and was No.40 in doubles and was experiencing homesickness and depression.

"I wanted to experience life as a normal teenaged girl and have some normal experiences," she said.

**"Her skill from the first time she picked up a bat was outstanding from a coach's perspective"**

Cricket and her didn't go looking for each other initially but it was definitely a case of "pleased to meet you" for both.

She was introduced to the national women's team early in 2015 to discuss her experiences as a professional athlete and was intrigued by what it would be like to play a team sport as a change from the individualism of tennis.

She had never picked up a bat competitively, having only played casually with her family. But when she approached Queensland Cricket about how she could get involved, Andy Richards, the coach of Women's National Cricket League team Queensland Fire and soon to be appointed to the women's Big Bash outfit Brisbane Heat, was instantly impressed.

"Her skill from the first time she picked up a bat was outstanding from a coach's perspective," he said. "She had never really picked up a real bat and faced a real ball — but when we chucked her into the nets and fed about 150 balls into the bowling machine she might have missed two and mis-hit maybe 10. I've not seen anything like it, before or since. What attracted me to her as a player was her ability to pick up things really quickly," he told the *Courier Mail.*

Barty began training with the Fire in July and also started playing with the Western Suburbs club which plays in Brisbane's women's Twenty20 league, scoring 63 from 60 balls and taking two wickets in her second appearance. She played 13 matches for the club, scoring one century and averaging 42.4 while taking eight wickets. Western Suburbs won the grand final with Barty top-scoring with 37 from 39 balls. In all, she made 545 runs at 30.28 for the club, taking eight wickets with off-spinners at 18.75.

The century and the grand final contribution made her pretty much a walk-up start for a $3000 contract with the Heat, a pittance compared to her tennis earnings, of course.

But that's where it got a bit harder. In her debut against the Melbourne Stars, she smashed 39 off 27 balls, her team's second highest score. A star had arrived, it seemed. However, a glance at cricket's stats bible, the *Crinfo* website, reveals that she played nine of the Heat's 14 matches, batting six more times for scores of 1, 7 not out, 0, 1, 17 and 3, for a total of 68 runs at an average of 11.3 and a strike-rate of 109.7, and did not bowl. On those numbers, it is fair to suggest she was never going to play for Australia — although Richards begs to differ. He wonders what might have been if she had stuck at it and still harbours hopes that she might return some day.

However, the experience was just what she was looking for.

Asked about it after her French Open triumph, she said: "It was truly an amazing period of my life. I met an amazing group of people who couldn't care less whether I could hit a tennis ball or not.

"They accepted me and they got to know Ash Barty. I still have those relationships. I got an amazing amount of messages over the last couple of days from those cricket girls who were some of my best friends.

"The way they are accepting of someone new coming into their locker room, into their dressing room and into their sport was amazing. They are truly an incredible group of girls that I know I'll have a relationship with for the rest of my life."

Team-mate Grace Harris, who was in the same tennis squad when they were younger and remembers a freakish player who was beating girls in grade nine and 10 when she was in grade one, said the cricket girls taught her not only how to celebrate but how to commiserate.

"After our last game of the season in Adelaide, we hit the town. Barty said, 'This would never happen in tennis. You get marching orders and notice when you have to vacate your apartment. You are on the next flight to the next competition. Then you have to find someone there you can have a hit with'.

"I said, 'welcome to a team sport'."

Another team-mate, Josie Fields, said the team learned a lot from her about being a professional athlete, with her dedication to fitness and rigorous training.

"It was the best thing she ever did, stepping away"

And a third one, Delissa Kimmince, said it was her humility that people admired the most. "When you know her, you know that she's such a down-to-earth girl," she told the *Sydney Morning Herald*. "It's nice to know that fame doesn't really change her. She's just Ash Barty from Ipswich and I have no doubt that's how she wants to be known."

Tyzzer, Barty's coach, said the switch in sports was critical to her subsequent tennis success. "It was the best thing she ever did, stepping away," he said. "She wanted to reassess her life. For someone to be able to step back in and play at the level she has after three years out is pretty amazing."

She remains an avid cricket fan, not only spending a day at Lord's during the one-day World Cup to watch Australia defeat England. When her Wimbledon match against Harriet Dart was over by lunchtime she dashed off to watch the Australian women's team play, renewing acquaintances with old team-mates and opponents.

That team went on to win their version of The Ashes, another significant addition to the fast-growing file of success stories in women's sport in Australia. No one applauded more enthusiastically than Barty.

11

# A CHUBBY LITTLE MISSILE LAUNCHER

Barty returned to tennis with no guarantees that she would have a meaningful future in it. She didn't even have a ranking and could, if you didn't know the real story, have been mistaken for just another battler trying her luck on the fringes of the circuit, hoping for the best but expecting nothing.

It had been a roller-coaster ride of a type pretty much unprecedented in Australian tennis.

But what had never been in any serious doubt — except perhaps in her own young head — was that she had the innate talent to get wherever she wanted to go.

It became obvious at a very early age.

She was not quite five when her parents took her to the West Brisbane Tennis Centre, having watched her hit a tennis ball against a wall with an old squash racquet almost from the time she could walk. Robert and Josie thought she might be ready to learn to play the game properly. They had no idea where this proclivity came from because no one in their families was remotely interested in the game.

In a pre-Wimbledon newspaper feature article tracing her

development, *Courier Mail* sportswriter Grantlee Kieza takes up the story: "Her first coach, Jim Joyce, says 'She was just a chubby little kid with a huge smile on her face'.

"Joyce's initial impression was that she was too young to join his classes but he decided to test her out. He tossed her a tennis ball. It flew back off her racquet like a fluorescent yellow missile.

"Thinking it was a fluke, he tossed her another. It flew past him even faster.

"Joyce told Ash's parents to bring her back next week.

"He made sure the little starlet lost her first proper match so she would not think success came too easily."

Joyce told Kieza: "Right from the start, her focus and concentration for a little kid were just phenomenal... I'd show her things and she'd pick them up straight away.

"Her biggest attribute wasn't just the hand to eye co-ordination — it was that she could listen and concentrate better than kids of 12 or 13. She was totally focussed on being a great player."

By the time she was 11 the prodigy was winning junior tournaments and was part of the Queensland Primary Schools team that won the 2007 Bruce Cup in Tasmania. In July 2008 she won the Queensland 12-years-old title and the following year received a $5000 grant from the Federal Government to help pay for a tennis trip to Perth.

At 14 she was Tennis Australia's junior athlete of the year

and was invited to Las Vegas as a guest of the Adidas player development team to receive specialist tuition from Andre Agassi's former coach, Australian Darren Cahill.

"Ash befriended Agassi's wife, tennis legend Steffi Graf, who passed on many tips," Kieza writes.

"Ash said the trip gave her confidence and self-belief and made her realise the sacrifices she needed to make to be a great tennis player."

**"Everyone was more excited than me, I just wanted to come home"**

The first real hint for the wider world that something special was brewing came in June 2011, when, aged 15, Barty made it through to the junior girls final at Wimbledon, where she faced the No.2 seed, Russia's Irina Khromacheva on the famed centre court.

Barty came from behind to take the first set 7-5 before opening up a 4-1 lead in the second, which eventually went to a tie-breaker, a pressure situation which she survived to claim the trophy — and the No.2 world ranking.

It was the biggest moment of her life but she simply offered a half-smile and a clenched fist in what passed for a celebration. "Everyone was more excited than me," she said. "I just wanted to come home." Which she immediately did, on the first available flight, for a family barbecue and a fishing trip. It was an early hint that the big wide world was not yet a comfort zone for her.

Not for the last time, Cawley was one of the first to send her a congratulatory message.

Six months later, she made her Grand Slam main draw debut at the Australian Open in Melbourne. She lost in the first round to Anna Tatishvili of Georgia, which she was happy to put down to experience. But former Davis Cup stalwart John Fitzgerald was already hailing her as "the best prospect we've had in 20 years in the women's game".

Another former star Jason Stoltenberg noted that she was not likely to be carried away by success. "There have been plenty of Wimbledon junior champions who fell by the wayside," he said. "Ash is doing well for a girl of 15 but we have to maintain perspective. She's still a young kid and she's barely scratching the surface of the game."

That wasn't lost on the kid herself.

Taking a break from school homework, she told Kieza: "Yes, I've won at Wimbledon but it's still only the juniors. It's just a stepping stone and there are still many more I have got to get over in the next few years."

# 12

# HOW TENNIS STOPPED BEING FUN AND BECAME A JOB

Ash Barty is not the first teenage sports star to find that life in the fast lane — especially when you're not emotionally ready for it, not as worldly-wise and not as used to dealing with inflated expectations and differentiating between Kipling's twin imposters, triumph and disaster, as you eventually become — is not as glamourous and exciting as everybody else perceives it to be. And she won't be the last. There are many cautionary tales about premature burnout.

These multiple pressures never sat well with Barty as she began to make her way in the world, often far from home, family and friends. Many of those close to her sensed it, but the extent of her discomfort never really became obvious — certainly not to the wider tennis community — until one day in in 2014, while still only 18, she announced simply that she was taking a break from professional tennis. After losing in the first round of the US Open, as she had done at the Australian and French tournaments, and ranked outside the top 200 in singles and 40 in doubles, she was mentally fatigued, saying she had been through too much too quickly from a young age and wanted "to experience life as a normal teenage girl and have some normal experiences".

Not much more was said then as she immersed herself in her new cricket career, but now that she is back in business in such a big way — with the world a much sunnier and more successful place — she has opened up freely on a number of occasions about her struggles to cope.

In one interview with sportswriter Craddock, she admitted she once cried her way through a match and into her coach's arms. "I tried to hide it as best I could for as long as I could," she said.

"Some days I felt normal, but others I'd feel I was incapable of anything. It's never, ever, ever been about the money. At the end of the day, it's very simple — I just didn't want tennis as a job."

For two years Barty took medication for depression and saw a therapist. They discussed how to manage a string of her "perfectionist" traits that involved small things like how she felt compelled to pack and unpack her bag the same way, Craddock wrote.

Her father Robert, himself a depression sufferer, strongly endorsed her decision to seek professional help. He and his wife had become aware that at one point they had seen her fewer than 40 days a year as she moved increasingly morosely from city to city, hotel room to hotel room.

Joyce, so close to her for so long as she became immersed in the game, was one of the first to spot the cracks. "She was unhappy all of 2014," he told Craddock. "Even though she was on the circuit and playing in the US Open and Wimbledon, she'd had enough.

"She was very upset. She was just cooked through the year. It was a gradual process. She showed the effects of it in 2014. After she won junior Wimbledon everyone got carried away, just the media and tennis Australia but her own expectation grew. We tried to keep it as level as we could but it was hard. Jason Stoltenberg said she was a victim of her own success."

As her sabbatical progressed, Barty stayed in touch with the sport by helping Joyce coach other young players and older women but when Wimbledon came around in 2015 she admitted that she had hardly bothered watching it on TV. Her disconnect was almost total.

Craddock noted that during her time out, she gained perspective on the privileges of her professional life. On idle walks she ran into school friends who were working at Woolworths or McDonalds to save money to go to university. In her last season, she had earned nearly $700,000.

"She went fishing, had a house built near her parents, played with her dogs and shared birthday dinners with her sisters. The smaller the treats the more she luxuriated in life's simple pleasures," Craddock wrote.

Joyce added: "She went back to being a normal person, going out with mates again. Even just a simple thing like going to the hotel with her friends. She liked that.

"She had never had the chance to do something like that.

She went to the races with me. Just acting normal."

And then, one day in early 2016, Barty's father returned home to five boxes of new tennis balls that had been left on the porch by a deliveryman.

Nothing had been said, but he knew what it meant.

She was back in business.

Or was she?

Craig Tyzzer wanted to know.

The Melbourne-based coach had worked with her briefly before she "retired" and was now about to become her full-time mentor at the behest of Stoltenberg, who had taken the reins from Joyce as she moved on from junior ranks.

A former circuit player between 1979 and 1983, Tyzzer is a low-profile but very experienced coach who won the Australian tennis award for high-performance coaching excellence in 2017, a year into his association with Barty.

According to tennis journalist Leo Schlink, he is "the type of character people gravitate to and lean on in troubled times".

When Barty approached him to say that she wanted to give tennis another go, he wanted to know one thing — how committed was she? Was she deadly serious? "The look she gave me, I knew she was pretty serious," Tyzzer told Schlink.

She was out of shape, he said, having done zero fitness work during the lay-off, but more than willing to make the necessary sacrifices which would start with a 12-week training block. Every day. In Melbourne, away from home.

"As soon as we were through the first week and she was exhausted I could see she was deadly serious," he said.

They decided to get through the first three months and then reassess, with Barty the perfectionist making it clear that if she was going to attempt this comeback she was determined to do it well. "I wanted to do it on my terms," she said.

Their return to the fray couldn't have been much more low-key, a lower-tier $50,000 tournament at Eastbourne, on the south coast of England, at a venue set among retirement

**"As soon as we were through the first week I could see she was deadly serious"**

villages – a world away in every sense from the last tournament in which she competed, the US Open in New York.

With no ranking she was accepted into the draw only because it wasn't full.

Tyzzer told his nervous but excited protégé: "This is where we start. Let's see where we're at."

He expected to get through a couple of matches at best, but she reached the semis in both singles and doubles. They moved on to the Nottingham tournament where she reached the quarters, but having played so little tennis she got bone stress from hitting so many balls and had to take a month off before she played again. After just two tournaments, the comeback had stalled but she wasn't worried — she was on her way.

On 6 June, she reappeared on the official rankings — at No.623. By the time 2016 finished, she had cut that almost in half, to 325.

The next year proved to be a real launching pad for her trip to the stars. She was quickly into stride, losing to world No.1 Angelique Kerber in the third round of the Brisbane International and then enjoying her best tilt at the Australian Open, reaching the third round. In March she won her first singles title in Kuala Lumpur and added the doubles with her old partner Casey Dellacqua.

She said at the time she had surprised herself with how well she was going. "It's a tribute to all the work we did in the off-season, and last year. It hasn't been quite 12 months since I started playing singles again. I'm certainly happy to be back."

Bouyed by two more doubles titles with Dellacqua, her close friend and confidant, she enjoyed a productive British grasscourt season, making the final at Birmingham — the tournament where she would later have one of her finest moments.

She reached the third round of the US Open, losing to the eventual champion Sloane Stephens, and then reached the final of the Wuhan Open in China, defeating three top 10 players but losing the decider to Caroline Garcia in three sets, which qualified her for the season-ending WTA Elite Trophy, which is contested by players ranked from nine to 20 who have not made the top-eight playoffs. There, she advanced out of her round robin group and was eliminated by one of her future doubles partners CoCo Vandeweghe, finishing the season with a career-high ranking of 17. She and Dellacqua also finished the year as the third highest ranked doubles team, winning three of six finals they contested and reaching the quarters or better at three of the four Grand Slams, including the French final.

On the strength of those performances, she comfortably won the end-of-year Newcombe Medal, Tennis Australia's best player award.

In her acceptance speech, she paid an emotional tribute to Dellacqua, who she said had been pivotal in getting her back in business. "Case, my best mate. She's not here tonight but I don't think she understands how much of a massive impact she has had on my life, bringing me back into the sport to be honest.

"She was the one who started the ball rolling again, to sort of finish that unfinished business in doubles and now we've been able to have a pretty amazing singles and doubles year.

"Case is my best friend, my mum on tour, my shoulder to cry on through many times and she helped me through my darkest days and has been able to share this year with me and really helped me through it the most. Case is probably the biggest thank you of all."

Things were falling into place nicely.

They continued to do so through 2018 with Barty making a strong start by reaching the final of the Sydney International in her second tournament of the year. Seeded at the Australian Open for the first time, at No.18, she fell to Osaka in the third round.

Seeded No.1 at a WTA event for the first time, she reached the semi-finals of the Internationaux de Strasbourg — her best result of the claycourt season — but had to retire with a back injury. The following week at the French Open, she lost to Serena Williams in the second round despite winning the first set.

Back on grass, she won the Nottingham Open for her second career WTA title, defeating local favourite and British No.1 Johanna Konta in the final. She then recorded her first wins at Wimbledon, matching her best result at a Grand Slam tournament. On hardcourts, she reached the semi-finals of the Canadian Open and the third round of the Cincinnati Open,

**"Case is my best friend, my mum on tour, my shoulder to cry on..."**

losing to world No.1 Simona Halep both times. Seeded 18 at the US Open, she reached the fourth round of a Grand Slam tournament for the first time, losing to No.8 Karolina Pliskova. But she then produced one of her career highlights to that point, winning the doubles with Vandeweghe.

She rounded off the year by falling one match short of repeating her progress to the final at Wuhan, but then winning the Elite Trophy, the best victory of her career and taking her ranking to another new high, 15.

Again, she won the Newcombe Medal, this time sharing it with rising male star Alex De Minaur.

By now, there was little, if any, doubt that she was on the cusp of genuine stardom. And so it proved.

13

# RULE NUMBER ONE: BE A NICE PERSON

After Wimbledon, with her precious new prizes — the French trophy and the No.1 ranking — safely in her possession, Barty returned home to Queensland to draw breath and prepare for the remainder of her extraordinary year, particularly the US Open in which many experts considered her an even better bet than she had been at either the French or Wimbledon because the hard surfaces suited her.

The homecoming she kept as low-key as possible, devoting it as always to family and friends. But there was no avoiding a hero's welcome when more than 100 kids arrived for a formal announcement that she would begin her new year with an appearance at the Brisbane International tournament in January.

She picked up a racquet and traded shots with the students for almost an hour, telling them that her new status had not changed her in any meaningful way. "Little things change but the way I live my life hasn't changed at all," she said. "I'm still exactly the same person. I just have a different number next to my name."

Naturally, the kids lapped it up, confirming that she was now Tennis Australia's best asset, by far, in terms of promoting the sport. The governing body said that her Paris heroics had generated a rise in interest, especially among girls and among children aged 5 to 12 in general. "The organisation's social media has also been flooded with comments from fans enthusing about their new-found role model," one report said, adding that the Fed Cup final tickets were selling faster than any such tie in history. Later in the year, Google confirmed her astonishing popularity by revealing that no Australian individual in any field had been researched more often.

In typically unfussed fashion, Barty told Newscorp's *Stellar* magazine: "The love and support I have received from Australians has gone to the next level. It's amazing. I can't wait for the Australian summer to come around."

On being a role model, she said: "If I can have an effect or a positive impact on one person's life, be it a young boy or girl or anyone in the world, that would be incredible. I am trying to share all the lessons I have learned and one of those is to really enjoy this. You can't take life so seriously, you have to be grateful for all of the positions you are put in.

"It's also about going about it the right way. Which is the way mum and dad taught me: sticking with my values, and my family's values." Jim Joyce's values too.

Reporter Jessica Halloran said the old coach gave his pre-teen pupil four rules to live by when she played the game. "First one?" he said. "Be a nice person. The second one is to respect people and be respected. Third one is to have fun. And the fourth one: if you can play tennis too, it's a bonus." It is safe to suggest the rules have all been observed to the letter.

# 14

# TOPPLED FROM THE TOP — BUT NOT FOR LONG

Barty returned to the fray, refreshed, at the Canadian Open for the start of the American hardcourt season, playing her first match on 7 August, one day less than exactly a month after her exit from Wimbledon.

She was rapidly brought back to earth, losing to 29$^{th}$ ranked American Sofia Kenin in three sets, which meant that her narrow points lead in the ranks would disappear if Naomi Osaka or Karolina Pliskova advanced far enough. Osaka won two matches before being despatched by Serena Williams in the quarters, which was enough for her to return to the top.

Barty's reign had lasted six weeks but that was still longer than Goolagong Cawley's two weeks back in 1976. And of course, who was to say she could not snatch it back as quickly as she surrendered it? Who, indeed!

She responded to what was a setback only in the perceptions of others with her usual class, saying that while she was disappointed she was not worried. As she had told the young fans at home: "It's just a number next to your name. It doesn't define you as a person or as a player. I'm certainly not going to lose any sleep over it."

She added: "It's not panic stations. It's my first match on a hardcourt in a long time." Returning to that surface for the first time since April, she had to cope with taping her shoulder to cope with the extra stress of hitting balls that bounced higher off the court. But there was no hint of an excuse.

Next up, Cincinatti, and an immediate opportunity to reclaim the ranking if she reached the final. This assignment started promisingly with a first-up straight-sets win over Russian superstar (if that's still a legitimate description of her) Maria Sharapova.

Things got tougher when Barty, by her own assessment playing "miles away" from her best, dropped the first set against both Anett Kontaveit of Estonia and Maria Sakkari of Greece before prevailing. Needing to win two tie-breakers against Kontaveit, Barty said the win said more about her willingness and ability to fight under pressure than her talent.

Russian veteran Svetlana Kutzenova over-powered her in straight sets in the semi-final, the No.1 still tantalisingly out of reach.

Accompanied by her boyfriend and parents, Barty arrived in New York for the Open saying she was more driven and hungry than ever for the last major of the year. She had no injuries and was "feeling good", and with encouraging memories of the previous year — when she progressed into the second week for the first time and won the doubles with Vandeweghe — she declared herself ready for "one more big push".

Her self-belief, reinforced by Crowe, who had joined her team after the previous year's Wimbledon, was by now tangible, noticeable by her positive demeanour in press conferences and other media engagements.

With Crowe's encouragement, she is not afraid to lay her ambitions on the line for all to see and hear, something a lot of athletes are not comfortable doing for fear of tempting fate or being accused of big-headedness.

"I think she has this beautiful balance of courage with consideration," Crowe told Newscorp's Jessica Halloran. "Courage to push herself out of her comfort zone and follow her dreams and goals.

"But she's also considerate so at the end of the day it is not all about her, but the impact she can have on someone else's life.

"She has said that publicly, if she can be a role model to another young boy or girl, to be a little bit braver, to have a bit more courage to push themselves, then that's success for her."

Again, Barty started uncertainly, winning only one game in the first set against Kazakhstan's Zarina Diyas before taking the first-round encounter comfortably in the end.

American Lauren Davis came and went in straight sets, as did Sakkari, leaving her one win away from a blockbuster encounter with Serena Williams. This was the same scenario that had confronted her at Wimbledon two months earlier, with the same result. The match-up never eventuated. "I only ever look at my next match," she said, noting that it was against China's Wang Qiang, the 18th seed and the highest-ranked rival she had encountered since downing Madison Keys in Paris.

Barty had beaten Wang in their two meetings the previous year but had to produce some of her best tennis to do it. This time, she made what turned out to be a controversial decision to play doubles on the rest day before the fourth-round showdown. She and her partner Victoria Azarenka won their second round match but were on court for nearly two and a half hours with the third set tie-breaker going to 12-10.

Wang rested.

No one will ever know for sure to what extent these starkly contrasting preparations were responsible for what ensued, which was a clear-cut, straight sets, 6-2 6-4, triumph for the Chinese star.

Barty clearly looked out of sorts, committing 39 unforced errors in 18 games, while being unable to convert any of nine break-point chances.

It is difficult to criticise her busy workload because doubles has always been important to her and she clearly enjoys it, never more than in this same tournament a year earlier, where she went all the way with Vandeweghe. This year, because Vandeweghe battled an ankle injury at the end of the previous year, Barty teamed up with Victoria Azarenka and almost pulled if off again, the pair losing 7-5 7-5 to third seeds Aryna Sabalenka and Elise Mertens. She also played doubles on the way to her French triumph, without any negative ramifications. Doubles is so much part of her routine that perhaps it helps her be the singles player that she is rather than compromising her main game, as some observers speculated.

Never one to dwell on defeat, Barty was as philosophical as ever after bowing out of the singles — referring, as usual, to her and her team with the collective pronoun "we".

**She was the only woman to reach the second week of all four majors**

"It's been incredible," she said at her media conference. "It's been a year where we've hit our goals. We've had a great season in Grand Slams for singles. We've made the second week in every single one, which has been really special. Now we'll sit back, reflect and look forward to a big couple of months to finish off the year.

"It's frustrating now. Again, give me an hour and I'll be right. It's an opportunity. It's a new day tomorrow. Just because we've had a tough hour and a half on court, it doesn't reflect on the year that I've had or the couple of weeks I've had here in New York."

The numbers confirmed just how special her year had been.

She was the only woman to reach the second week of all four majors, her consistency matching her class. She won 17 of those matches and lost only three. Overall, by the time she departed New York she had won 45 matches in 2019, an equal tour-best, and had lost only 11 matches in the 12 months since the previous year's US Open.

And in the end, she departed New York a winner after all.

Because Osaka lost in the fourth round to Switzerland's Belinda Bencic, the No.1 ranking changed hands again — it was back with Barty.

Lleyton Hewitt, in 2001 and 2002, is the only Australian player to have ever finished the year at No.1, although obviously Laver and others would have done so if the rankings had existed before 1973, when they were introduced.

But because she had a healthy lead over her two closest rivals, Osaka and Pliskova, and because she had fewer points to defend as the season entered it's final stages in China, she had that feat firmly in her grasp.

The two tournaments there, the Wuhan Open and the China Open, were highly productive — she reached the semi-finals in the first one, beaten by Belarus's Aryna Sabalenka in straight sets, and got to the final of the other one, where Osaka prevailed in three sets — but they also suggested a long, hard year was starting to take its toll.

That shouldn't have come as any great surprise given that she had won more matches than any other woman on the circuit while earning at a rate of better than a million dollars a month and having to deal with increased media interest and other off-court obligations.

As they say, nobody ever said it would be easy at the top. The Beijing event, the last of the year's premier mandatory tournaments, saw her having to survive three consecutive three-set matches, all lasting more than two hours, to reach the final. There, she started well against the Japanese star, winning the first set — but then fatigue set in as her serve faltered and the unforced error count mounted, going down 3-6 6-3 6-2 in just under two hours.

That meant the immediate past No.1 and the incumbent one were now level at 2-2 in head-to-head combat, prompting suggestions that the game might be seeing the formation of an epic rivalry into the immediate future.

The succession of long, difficult matches didn't faze Barty. Nothing much does. "I think the best part about it is I enjoy these moments," she said. "I enjoy when it's tight, when your back is against the wall. That really brings out the fun for me."

She said it had provided her with "a massive growth" in her mental fortitude when she faced crunch points. And it wasn't just her tennis that was benefiting.

"It's for my life, my health, my well-being as well, which has been the best thing," she said. "I have never been happier on the court. It's been a brilliant time in my life."

Barty left Beijing, bound for Melbourne in time to collect her Hall of Fame gong and for a well-earned rest before the season-ending championships back in China still with an almost unassailable lead in the rankings.

Still where she belongs — and where she obviously intended to be for some time yet.

On top of the world.

# 15

# IT'S WE NOT ME — THE ONE WORD THAT DEFINES THE ASH BARTY THAT I KNOW

BY LINDA PEARCE

There was no mention of her name. Not that time. Not when former doubles great and Davis Cup hero John Fitzgerald, then a Tennis Australia board member, declared in a 2010 radio interview that the nation had unearthed its best women's prospect in a generation.

Within tennis circles, her identity was no secret. As I wrote back then, that futile attempt at anonymity would therefore neither fail to dampen expectations nor protect the innocent: an exquisitely-talented 14-year-old named Ashleigh Barty.

But did the hope that would become hype seem justified at the time? One of the opinions sought was from Scott Draper, then Tennis Australia's national head coach. It was compelling.

Comparable court craft to long-time No.1 Martina Hingis, said the former top 50 player, but with potentially more power. Similarities of style with the sublime shot-maker and four-time major winner Hana Mandlikova, but with a bigger serve.

So gifted, Draper enthused. Such hand-eye co-ordination.

Skill and touch. Able to volley and slice. "But it's a long road, and we have a history in this country lately of making kids feel like they've made it before they actually have, and that's certainly not what we intend to do," he said.

"Yes, there's going to be hype around her, and yes, there's excitement that there's someone there who's as good as she is and is ticking as many boxes as she is, but it's a journey and you never really know until they're on the tour, day in and day out, competing against the best in the world."

So now we're sure. Have been for a while. In 2019, nine years and one lengthy interval later, the reigning French Open champion would playfully reference Disney films *The Lion King*, *Toy Story* and *The Little Mermaid* while holding court in the prestigious main interview room at the All England Club as the world No.1 and Wimbledon top seed. This was not a movie scene, at least not yet, but there has already been a happy ending.

In her own time, and way, the diminutive girl who had been hailed as Australia's Next Big Thing had grown up into the player whose results matched that prodigious potential, and whose now-famous name was already synonymous with unaffected humility, respect and grace.

A throwback, of sorts, too. Not just through the skin colour and so-called "squishy" little nose that harks back to her paternal great, great grandmother's indigenous heritage, but also to the country's golden tennis age, when champions were loved and admired — as much for their sportsmanship and demeanour as their achievements.

Pat Rafter had his trademark "sorry mate" when

> **"When she's playing instinctively and she's comfortable, she sees the court a little bit differently to most other players"**

apologising to an opponent for an errant ball toss. "Too good, mate," Barty would happily say when beaten by a better opponent on the day.

Yet before and after that marvellously instinctive 'what the f...?' reaction after match point in her finals drubbing of Marketa Vondrousova in the final at Roland Garros, the most remarked-upon word in her vocabulary remains one of the smallest: we.

The collective pronoun is Barty's way of including and acknowledging the supportive team around her, including Tyzzer, strength and conditioning guru Mark Taylor, performance coach Ben Crowe and agent Nikki Craig.

Way back in my personal catalogue of Barty's career is a story written in 2012, when the 15-year-old fresh from sweeping through the 18-and-under-nationals and just having beaten Casey Dellacqua in the round-robin stage of the Australian Open wildcard play-off did an almost painfully short and shy interview with a handful of Melbourne-based reporters beside an outside court.

And yes, there it was: "We didn't really have a game plan." We.

Still, what this unique individual has always had was the game, both technically and tactically, an innate competitiveness, and natural gifts enhanced by hard work. "When she's playing instinctively and she's comfortable," says her former coach Jason Stoltenberg, "she generally sees the court a little bit differently to most other players."

Back in 2012, he had spoken sagely of Barty as "an emotional talent and building to handle pressure". He warned that she would need to be managed carefully. And that the rest of us would need to maintain perspective. Winning the Wimbledon juniors had been both blessing and curse, it has since been acknowledged. An incredible honour, yet way too soon. Everyone was more excited than an "absolutely cooked" Barty, who skipped the posh Champions' Ball to come straight home, but arrived to a reception at Brisbane Airport that her sister Ali recalls as "crazy".

It was all overwhelming for a teenager who had started with an old wooden racquet and a garage wall, as a tomboy wearing her favoured outfit of board shorts, t-shirt and backwards cap. Netball was for girls, apparently, including her big sisters, Sara and Ali. Hockey would have been OK though. At least they used sticks.

Then she found tennis. And, via a family recommendation, met local coach Jim Joyce.

The newcomer was a natural from that first visit to the modest West Brisbane Tennis Centre, still about two weeks out from her fifth birthday. Despite his initial protests that he didn't take on children before the age of seven or eight, Barty won Joyce over, almost instantly, that first day on court four.

It was more than just the remarkable hand-eye co-ordination that did it, for there was intense focus and concentration, keenness, the fact she hung off every word. The tiny newcomer was even the first to start picking up the balls afterwards. Yes, Joyce famously said: "Darling, you can come back next weekend."

"... that's her coach – does he think we're stupid?"

So much of this element of the story is already part of the Barty legend, for Joyce has been a proud and happy-to-chat-to-anyone-who-asks mentor from day one. He made it his mission to equip Barty with all the tools, from the backhand slice to the kick serve she had to build the strength to deliver, the volleying skills, touch, variety.

So it was that each week after she clambered out of the family Ford for her lesson at the unpretentious facility in an industrial precinct that would never be mistaken for Royal South Yarra, winning took its own back seat to learning. Which, at the same time, was considered less important than being a decent person, and remains far less of a priority than being a role model and example.

At the same time, Joyce describes himself as Barty's

"handbrake her whole life". He was the coach who limited her private lessons, then her time spent playing against kids her own age, fostered her love of tennis, varying her practice and the ages of her hitting partners, caring less about what others were doing than sticking to the Barty blueprint for success he knew would come when the time was right.

One trophy was thrown in the bin by Joyce, only half in jest, as a way of stressing that the later ones would be the ones that mattered. Others were donated back to local clubs and associations to be rebadged with new engraving plates. Not Barty's trash, but sure to be treasured elsewhere.

There was the time Joyce advised the parents of one of Barty's opponents to exploit her weakness against low forehands. It was during a period of ill-advised — but mercifully brief — flirtation with an extreme Western-style grip favoured by the likes of Rafael Nadal.

An incredible yearning and aptitude for learning opened up too many possibilities, sometimes. "One day she was playing a final at the Coops Tennis Centre, and after the semi-finals the parents of the other kid she had to play in the final were there talking to the Bartys, and they introduced me and they said 'you're doing a great job with Ash or something', and the Bartys said 'yeah, she's going well'," said Joyce.

He proceeded to tell them to play to Barty's weakness, which was then low and short on the forehand side. "And then I walked away. Anyway, the parents said to the Bartys, 'that's her coach — does he think we're stupid? That we're going to listen to that?' They said, 'no, no, he's fair dinkum. He wants her to have practice. He wants to prove to her that that's her weakness and also to practise that shot'."

By the time Barty hit double-figures in age, with her national ranking already soaring, she was practising several times a week against men. Decent players, too. "They'd say how do you want us to play against her?," Joyce recalls.

"I'd say 'look, don't go full bore, just push her as hard as what you think she can handle', and most of them would come back to me and go 'boy, she can take a fair bit, this kid'. They were amazed, for a little girl, because she wasn't very big, Ash."

Nor was Justine Henin, Joyce's poster-girl and a pin-up for the short-of-stature types with deceptive power and all the shots. And also fiercely, fiercely competitive. Enough said.

Barty is big now, in another sense. Yet she wasn't, not so much, on this particular day we were sitting beside a clay court.

It was almost 17,000km from the famous one in Paris named for Philipe Chatrier, which Barty would never have imagined as the scene of her first grand slam singles title. Instead, the backdrop was one of eight Italian clay courts at Melbourne's National Tennis Centre, and Barty had recently spent most of her 17$^{th}$ birthday on a flight from Dubai to Sydney.

Chatting in her usual understated fashion before practising that morning, there was less of a premonition of what might soon go wrong for the 2011 junior Wimbledon champion as a hint of what, six years later, would turn out so marvellously right.

The previous month in Switzerland, Barty had become

the youngest Australian since Jelena Dokic to win a Fed Cup match. The achievement prompted captain and former world No.8 Alicia Molik to predict that clay would eventually be the reluctant Queenslander's best surface.

Barty could joke that those were not words she was keen to hear, for she had grown up on hardcourts and considered grass her most natural habitat. Clay, well, not so much. Yet Molik was not the first to see the possibilities; the fact that her most junior team member's creativity, versatility and variety would be well-suited to a surface that rewards power and patience, graft and guile.

What wasn't forecast on that sunny May day, though, was how dark everything would soon become for the homebody from Ipswich, the baby of a close-knit, animal-loving family with dogs (or puppies, as she prefers to call Chino and Affie — a coffee lover's names — plus Rudy and Maxi), cats and birds. An assertive child would nevertheless crave the normality that her prodigious sporting skills would serve to thwart.

It was less than 12 months later that some of those closest to Barty could see the cracks appearing. She was way ahead of schedule in a tennis sense, having banked a cheque for almost $150,000 after an Australian Open debut that included a doubles final appearance with Dellacqua, then contested a maiden WTA singles quarter-final in Malaysia before accepting a French Open wildcard and reaching the doubles decider there, too.

She could smile as she described her belated birthday celebration in suburban Springfield: a quick dinner, then home to watch the footy on the couch. Which was just how the fanatical Richmond supporter liked it, even if a truly perfect day might have included a spot of fishing, too. Or "wetting a line", as her famous friend and mentor, Evonne Goolagong Cawley, likes to say.

Barty could speak honestly about being a no-fuss teenager who eschewed attention, one who was happiest going about quietly in her hoodie. She could joke about not rushing to get herself a car, being an L-plater who didn't drive anywhere because she was always travelling, and not needing to buy a house because her parents Josie and Robert already had one of those.

Barty was a kid with a special gift that had not prepared her where it would take her — so far away, often, and for such long, lonely stretches, but also one dealing with mental health issues. Less than 16 months later, this same reporter would write a story on 19 September 2014, headlined "Ashleigh Barty gives no hint of return after walking away from tennis".

Shockingly, but necessarily, an indefinite hiatus had begun.

Much has been written about what happened next (e.g. the stint playing Women's BBL cricket for the Brisbane Heat, the chance to refresh and enjoy the life of "a normal chick" she had craved, the non-tennis friends she made, the time at home she savoured).

Or what didn't happen (missing tennis, at least not in the beginning, while still coaching with Joyce for shop assistant wages and being allocated the worst jobs — the ones he

> "... 'Oh God, this isn't working!'"

thought she would like the least. The theory: perhaps then she would appreciate how extraordinary her tennis-playing life had been, and the possibilities that remained if she returned).

"She was coaching old ladies and going 'this is good fun', and I was going, 'What is wrong with her?'," Joyce said, in a long phone interview in late 2017. "I'd be giving her the junior kids on the end court and she'd be coming up with a smile on her face and my sister-in-law said, 'How long's Ash gonna keep doing this for?' and I said, 'Oh, it can't be too much longer!'

"She was going to schools for me and I was getting her to do all these jobs like 'pick up this for me, Ash'. I paid her $40 an hour or something because I didn't want her to think 'oh, I'm on a couple of thousand a week now, I can sit back and do nothing'. But then she started doing a few private lessons and going, 'Oh this is good', and I was, 'Oh God, this isn't working!'

"Wimbledon 2015 she's doing a holiday clinic with me and I mentioned Wimbledon to her and she said, 'Oh I looked at it a little bit, Mum and Dad had it on, I'm not really interested'. And I've gone, 'Oh, gawd, this is not going good'."

Here was where golf, too, entered the narrative. Her parents Robert and Josie were both keen golfers when they met, and a lovely story her father — a former scratch golfer and former state and national representative — told me a few years back was of

Ash deciding to try that sport during her time away from tennis.

Barty senior insists he had not given her any tips, and was an unwilling teacher who simply accompanied his daughter — and her shiny new clubs — to the Brookwater Golf Club and sat in on the meeting where the club pro asked what she hoped to achieve. Answer: just to be able to hit the ball and play an OK round.

Next question: how much had she played? Three times. What did she shoot? The last, time at Gailes Golf Club, south of Brisbane, was an 85. Which, said the pro encouragingly, wasn't bad for nine holes. Except, Barty junior said, it was for 18.

"He said 'are you for real'? And I just started laughing. I said look, take her out'," Rob Barty recalled. "So he took her up to the driving range and said, 'Look, here's a wedge, I want you to try and aim it towards that first flag down there' and she's hit the first three shots to within 10 feet of the pin. He just looked at me and I said, 'Don't look at me! She is annoying'."

Years earlier, Barty had also noticed his youngest child watching the cricket on TV. Think of that kid who has loads of friends despite not just being good at everything, but really good, good. That was Ash. "I can remember her watching Shane Warne bowl on the television and one day she called me outside and said, 'Hey, look, Dad, I can bowl like Warnie', and she could bowl a leg spinner." Just like that. A glimpse into the future. Perhaps.

Still, the elite cricket element may have been overplayed slightly in the re-telling of the Barty story, for she was not the next Ellyse Perry, and did not — as is so often reported — give up tennis to play in the Women's Big Bash League. Rather, after being invited to address the Australian women's team in Brisbane during her break from tennis, she decided to spend the summer of 2014-15 trying something new and more collaborative.

The greatest impact came through her immersion in, and enjoyment of, the team environment, having known only an individual sport. For the first time, she enjoyed a beer at the end of the day, and the bonding experience on a team camp with the Brisbane Heat.

Sport could be different to the way she had lived it as Tennis Prodigy Barty 1.0 and, in that respect, the importance of cricket can not be underestimated. Yet Barty insists that handling the long stretches away from the home she built five minutes' drive from her parents is no easier than it ever was; it's more that, at 23, her management and perspective have improved.

Back in the day, Rafter set up house in the tax haven of Bermuda, Lleyton Hewitt based himself in the Bahamas, and Sam Stosur is one of the many to have a residence in Florida. Pat Cash still calls London home. While the benefits of convenience and the financial bottom line mean it can never be ruled out, who can imagine taking Barty out of Ipswich? Not Ash, anyway.

Thus, while Nadal slipped back to nearby Majorca after the French Open to rest before the grass court season, and Roger Federer made the even shorter schlep to Switzerland, Team Barty took the Eurostar to England for welcome downtime that included a few rounds at the former Ryder Cup course, The Belfry, in Warwickshire. The nine-handicapper was joined by Tyzzer, her parents, and Kissick, the resident pro at the aforementioned Brookwater Club.

When the coach tweeted a picture with his smiling charge on one of the lush greens, it prompted my friendly reminder to Tyzzer that he and Rob Barty had vowed some time ago that they would no longer play golf with the multi-sports star, because she would beat them — off the men's tees.

So, who won this time? "She took my money again," came the predictable reply. Of course she did. Too good, mate.

> **"Her fitness was proving far more 'brutal' than her touch"**

Tyzzer, a mature, calm father of daughters, has proved to be the ideal fit. Just as Joyce chose to pass the baton to Stoltenberg when he felt he could take the rising star no further, Tyzzer was also hand-picked. Rob Barty is convinced that if the trio were to have their voices masked during a collective discussion about his daughter and her game, the words would be so similar it would be impossible to tell them apart.

In 2016, with the Tyzzer-Barty collaboration still in its infancy, the three of us shared a table at a cafe on Swan Street in Richmond, Melbourne — Barty just three tournaments into her comeback, but already ranked 5th in Australia and 304th in the world.

Tyzzer was, as he remains, a positive, reassuring presence, having just overseen a demanding training block with fitness coach Narelle Sibte. Barty was admitting that her fitness was proving far more "brutal" to regain than her touch.

Fast forward to just over a year later, when we are all in China at the Wuhan Open, and a noticeably sleeker, stronger Barty beats three top 10 players to reach the final. It is a strong field, and another big step for the player about to debut in the top 30.

It is also AFL Grand Final week. Reluctantly, Barty has to settle for some long-distance viewing, and after reaching her biggest career final to date declares to this habitually disappointed Melbourne supporter as we discuss long-distance viewing options: "Hopefully tennis doesn't get in the way tomorrow!" This day, it would be France's Caroline Garcia who intervenes.

The year closes with the WTA Elite Trophy in Zhuhai — the celebration limited to a quiet beer in the tournament hotel with Tyzzer and great friend and doubles partner Dellacqua. We chat after Barty is home and, asked to rate her year, the world No.17 declares it "as close to 10 out of 10 as it gets".

Reminded of this 12 months later, a bemused Tyzzer remarks drily that it rather limits the scope for improvement. His score: eight out of 10 and, for 2018 (year-end ranking, consolidated at No.15) probably an 8.5. "The good part is I don't think she's reached her full potential yet. There's still room for improvement, and Ash knows that and she's working fully on those areas."

No argument about the progress, though, and what seemed to inevitably lie ahead, both pre-2014 and soon into the post-2016 second stage confirmed at a Dellacqua barbecue where Barty remembers realising: "I'm ready, here. Good to go". And good to stay, for the past had been dealt with, even if Joyce had despised the fact a young teenager had been the subject of such best-in-a-generation hype.

"I hated all that back then when all those guys were saying that. We were the opposite; we were trying to play it down, and I don't care how good someone is at 12 — you can't say that. Look at (Bernard) Tomic, look at all of them. It doesn't just happen. You've got to let 'em find their feet, and let 'em become what they become."

**"The good part is I don't think she's reached her full potential"**

If there has been a more popular Australian tennis player since the beloved Rafter, then sorry, mate, but they're impossible to name. Which is no slight on Stosur, who has been more inscrutable, so often screened by sunglasses, and different in so many ways. No less admirable or likeable but a vastly different style of player and perhaps slightly more difficult for the masses to get to know.

Stosur also struggled to convert her momentous success at Flushing Meadows, where she shocked the great Serena Williams in the 2011 final, and that sustained French Open excellence, where she has reached the semis four times and was a finalist in 2010, into the singles results she so dearly wanted to achieve at home.

Barty's pre-2019 Australian Open best was her round-of-16 loss to eventual finalist Petra Kvitova. But it also acted as a springboard for a remarkable season in which she claimed the prestigious Miami Open on hardcourt two months before the French, with a grass court title in Birmingham that clinched the No.1 ranking soon afterwards.

Goolagong Cawley had been the last Australian woman to reach the summit, and Barty's pal, fellow fisherwoman and Indigenous example was in Brisbane in April, when not only was the bandwagon already full-to-overflowing, but it was all aboard the Barty Bus.

A real one. Seriously. For the Easter Fed Cup tie against Belarus, there was a free, specially-decorated charter service organised to ferry ticket-holders the 40km from Ipswich to Pat Rafter Arena.

"I saw it and I was like 'what's going on?'" Barty laughed in a pre-tie phone interview. "But, no, very cool. Any way that we can get more people into the stands here is awesome." An Australian Fed Cup record crowd of 5126 was duly set at Tennyson — only to be exceeded in the final against France in Perth.

The Australian Open was still played at suburban Kooyong the last time a home-grown man or woman won the national title, and if the obscure answer to that trivia question is Chris O'Neil, then there are some irresistible clues to the identity of her natural successor.

She's the proud Australian who travels with a yellow Sherrin she uses in warm-ups; made sure to check the World Cup cricket scores during her momentous run at Roland Garros; and walked on for her must-win Fed Cup reverse singles against world No.10 Aryna Sabalenka carrying her three-year-old niece Lucy, like it was just any other Sunday chilling out in her Queensland backyard.

The one whose trophies are multi-purposed as vases by her mum and sisters; who reserves Friday nights at home for family dinners (chicken curry, ideally); is known as Auntie Ash at the local kindergarten and elsewhere; and insists on spoiling her family, because she wants to, and can.

The player who sent her father and first coach text messages about how thrilled she was to have reached the top 100 says the only thing that has changed is that single-digit next to her name, returns home to affection and appreciation after beating the world's best, and embodies all that Australians like to love in their sporting elite.

Yes, happily, there is no problem naming her now. Too good, mate, indeed.

16

# TIMELINE TO THE TOP

## CHRIS McLEOD TRACES THE RISE AND RISE OF TENNIS'S NEWEST SUPERSTAR

**NAME:** Ashleigh Barty

**BORN:** Wednesday 24 April 1996

**HEIGHT:** 1.66 m (5 ft 5 in)

**NATIONALITY:** Australian. Indigenous heritage.

**TENNIS:** Right-handed all-courter (two-handed backhand).

**DESCRIBES HERSELF:** Fun. Passionate. Dedicated.

**THE START:** Ash joined the International Tennis Federation (ITF) junior girls tour, a worldwide competition for under-18 junior tennis players, in 2009. In her first singles event she reached the second round at Waikato Bays ITF and The New Zealand 18 and Unders Indoor Championship.

**PROFESSIONAL:** Turned professional in April 2010 just after her 14th birthday, at an ITF $25,000 event in her hometown of Ipswich, losing her first match 4-6 5-7 to another Australian, Karolina Wlodarczak.

**FIRST PRO MATCH WIN:** Mt Gambier ITF tournament, 12 October 2010; in her second professional tournament appearance defeated Ayu-Fani Damayanti of Indonesia 6-7 6-3 6-3. She reached the semi-finals before bowing out. She went on to win two ITF Junior titles in Queensland; she reached the final of a third but lost.

**FIRST BIG-STAGE WIN:** 2011 Junior Girls Wimbledon title, defeating Russian Irina Khtomacheva 7-5 7-6.

**GRAND SLAM MAIN DRAW DEBUT:** Australian Open, 2012, losing 2-6 6-7 to Anna Tatishvili of Georgia.

**FIRST WOMEN'S TENNIS ASSOCIATION (WTA) TITLE:** Malaysian Open 2017.

**STRENGTHS:** Kicking serve and deft sliced backhand compensate for slight stature. Solid groundstrokes on both forehand and backhand sides. Able to find the corners and lines with pin-point accuracy. Uses her powerful forehand to create sharp angles on cross-court shots. Not afraid to close in on the net. Has won on all three major surfaces — grass, clay and hardcourt. At one point in 2010, Ash had a win/loss record of 30-2. She got to No.2 in the world on the junior circuit.

By 2012, Ash was in the top 200 women players, aged just 16. By 17, she had posted her first singles win in a

Grand Slam. That year she also won her first Grand Slam doubles match. Ash finished the 2018 season fourth on the WTA Tour for aces served — 297, averaging almost five per match. She was second in percentage of service points won in 2018 by a player with at least 10 matches, behind only Serena Williams.

Ash's technical ratings by Tennis Australia Game Insight Group (GIG) Player DNA report: Out of a best possible score of 100 — 89.0 for serve, 86.3 for forehand, and 90.9 for backhand, putting her in the top 10 of active players on overall technical ability.

**COMMUNITY:** Ash is National Indigenous Ambassador for Tennis Australia, promoting more indigenous participation in tennis. She is also an ambassador for the RSPCA.

**ENDORSEMENTS:** Fila, Rado, Jaguar, Kayo Sports, Head, Vegemite, Banana Boat and Esmi.

**CAREER EARNINGS:** Approximately $AUD 34 million at 31 July 2021 ($USD 25 million, including endorsements worth $USD 4 million), ranked three in world women's sport behind Naomi Osaka (highest earning female sports star of all time) and Serena Williams (estimates by Forbes).

**WIN/LOSS RECORD:** To 31 July 2021 —

Singles — 287/100 (ranked 1 in singles).

Doubles — 195/63 (ranked 36 in doubles).

# 17

# MATCH POINTS IN THE CAREER OF ASH BARTY

**2009:** Joins the International Tennis Federation junior girls circuit aged 13.

**2010:** Plays her first tournaments on the ITF Australian circuit; wins two Junior titles in Queensland and reaches the final of a third.

**2011:** Wins ITF Junior titles in Thailand, Malaysia and Belgium. Wins Wimbledon junior crown at 15 years of age, seeded 12, dropping just one set on the way. Gets a wildcard entry into qualifying at the US Open but misses out on the main draw. Finishes year as No.2 junior. Member of Australia's winning Junior Fed Cup team.

**2012:** Makes Women's Tennis Association (WTA) debut at the Brisbane International and secures a wildcard for her first Grand Slam event, the 2012 Australian Open. As part of the ITF Futures Pro Tour Circuit in 2012, she claims her first tour win at home, in Sydney, and followed up with wins in Mildura and Nottingham. She wins a total of eight (including four doubles) tournaments for the season, a highlight being a win in the ITF Toyota title in Toyota, Japan, over fellow Australian Casey Dellacqua, with whom she goes on to form a successful doubles partnership. As well as the Australian Open, she makes the main draws of the French Open and Wimbledon but doesn't get past the first round in all three.

**2013:** Makes her Fed Cup debut for Australia at 16, the youngest to do so since Jelena Dokic in 1998. Wins Grand Slam first-round matches at the French Open and US Open to climb to career-high ranking of No.129. Reaches Grand Slam doubles finals with Casey Dellacqua at Australian Open, Wimbledon and US Open. Ash and Casey win the Birmingham Classic in the U.K, Ash's first WTA-level tournament win. Finishes the year ranked No.12 in doubles, the only teenager in the top 20.

**2014:** Suffers an injury at the Brisbane International; she plays in three of the four Grand Slams but loses all her opening matches. In doubles, she and Casey win their second tournament and make it to the quarter-finals of the French Open and Wimbledon. Announces in September after US Open that she is taking an "indefinite break" from tennis.

**2015:** Tries cricket. Signs with the Brisbane Heat to play in the inaugural Cricket Australia Women's Big Bash League.

**2016:** Returns to pro tennis on the ITF circuit, making the final of four tournaments and wins three but mostly plays doubles. On the WTA Tour she reaches the quarter-finals of the Nottingham Open and the second round of qualifying for Wimbledon.

**2017:** Starts the year at No.232 and finishes at No.17, first time in the top 20. Wins her first Women's Tennis Association singles title, in Malaysia. Becomes Australia's No.1 woman player. Reaches first WTA doubles final — the French Open — with Casey Dellacqua. They win the Birmingham Classic doubles and reach the finals of the Eastbourne International and the Connecticut Open. They qualify for their first appearance at the season-ending WTA Doubles Championship, losing in the quarter-finals. Finishes with 30-15 win/loss record in singles.

**2018:** Collects three WTA titles: singles in Nottingham and the WTA Elite Trophy in Zhuhai, China, then the US Open doubles (with American Coco Vandeweghe). Reaches the third round of the Australian Open, second round of the French Open and the fourth round of the US Open where she loses in three sets to Serna Williams. Ranked No.15 in singles and No.7 in doubles. Best win is over world No.3 Angelique Kerber at Wuhan. Has 46-19 win/loss record in singles.

**2019:** Wins three WTA singles titles in six months – Miami, French Open (her first Grand Slam) and Birmingham on her way to No.1 and on to Wimbledon. Her early exit from Wimbledon means she loses the No.1 spot. Ranks No.2 in US Open. Regains world No.1 on 9 September after the US Open when other contenders fail to reach the semi-finals. Confirmed at No.1 after reaching semi-final at Wuhan Premier 5 event in late September. First to qualify for the WTA singles finals play-offs in the Porsche Race to Shenzhen, China, for the top 8 ranked players at the end of the year. Completes the Beijing Open, the last "major" before the WTA finals, still as World No.1, and though losing the Beijing final to Osaka in three sets, she retains a clear lead in the rankings pointscore with a strong claim to be world No.1 at the end of the year.

18

# 2019: ON TOP OF THE WORLD

Ash headed for Shenzhen and the WTA year-end championship already the winner of the 2019 Porsche Race to Shenzhen, for which the prize was a Porsche car for being No. 1 at the end of the regular season.

Each of the 56 tournaments (52 WTA events plus the four Grand Slams) before the Shiseido WTA Finals Shenzhen represented one lap on the Porsche Race to Shenzhen, spread across 29 countries and regions.

Ash collected 6,476 points from 14 laps (i.e. tournaments), with nearest rival Karolina Pliskova second with 5,315 points.

"It was already an honour to qualify for the WTA Finals, but to also finish the Porsche Race to Shenzhen on top is an achievement I'm incredibly proud of," Ash said. "This is a special tournament for myself and my team and I'll be fighting hard to finish the WTA season with the Shenzhen title."

And she succeeded, defeating Elina Svitolina 6-4, 6-3 in the series-ending finale contested be eight of the world's elite players. On the way there in the round robin group format, she defeated Belinda Bencic 5-7, 6-1, 6-2; lost to Kiki Bertens 6-3, 3-6, 4-6;

defeated Petra Kvitova 6-4, 6-2; and defeated Karolina Pliskova 4-6, 6-2, 6-3.

Ash had not beaten Svitolina in five meetings before Shenzhen. But she dominated the defending champion on the indoor court with her heavy, forceful forehand, attacking behind it.

Ash's victory ended Svitolina's 10-match winning streak at the WTA Finals.

As well as cementing her place at the top of the world rankings, Ash's winning cheque was to that time the biggest in the history of tennis (men and women) for a championship.

She followed Evonne Goolagong Cawley who was WTA champion in 1976.

Just 23 at the time, Ash had claimed four titles — Roland Garros, WTA Finals, Miami Open and Birmingham — on all four surfaces and winning 56 matches.

In something of an understatement, she said: "It's been the most incredible year for me."

Ash's 2019 achievements included:

- Winning her first Premier Mandatory title at the Miami Open.
- Claiming her first Grand Slam singles title at the French Open.
- Winning the Birmingham title to rise to world No. 1 for the first time.
- Finishing the year as the world's top player.
- Most wins for the year on the women's tour — 56.
- Best record of wins against top 10 players — 12.

- Becoming the fifth player to win the WTA Finals on debut.
- Becoming the first world No. 1 to win the WTA Finals series since Serena Williams in 2014.
- Winning titles on all four playing surfaces — indoor, grass, clay and hardcourt.
- Claiming the biggest champion's cheque in the history of tennis, taking home $US 4.42 million for her week at the elite eight-player finals tournament in Shenzhen.
- Ranked No. 1 in world women's tennis at year-end.

19

# 2020: THE LOST YEAR

The tennis world waited with great expectation to see how Ash Barty's defence of her World No. 1 ranking unfolded through 2020.

Could she stay No. 1, could she retain her French Open title, could she win another slam, could she take the Wimbledon crown?

In what turned out to be an annus horribilis for sport at all levels, from social to elite and in between, tennis was one of many sports that took a significant pummelling from the Coronavirus pandemic. Many tennis tournaments were cancelled or postponed, including the Tokyo Summer Olympics that were rescheduled to 2021.

Ash Barty should have been living the dream in 2020. She was world No. 1 after her stellar 2019 year and season-end championship.

She was looking to defend her French crown and redress last year's early exit at Wimbledon. The Olympic Games in Tokyo were firmly in sight from the end of June to the end of July.

Times were particularly tough for Australians seeking to

plot their way around world events. Overseas travel was severely impacted and even closed borders within Australia became a problem.

Ash decided not to tour: "It has been a difficult decision to make but unfortunately I will not be competing in Europe this year. Last year's French Open was the most special tournament of my career so this is not a decision I have made lightly.

"There are two reasons for my decision. The first is the health risks that still exist with Covid. The second is my preparation, which has not been ideal without my coach being able to train with me due to the state border closures in Australia.

"I wish the players and the French Federation all the best for a successful tournament.

"I now look forward to a long pre-season and the summer in Australia. It has been a challenging year for everyone and although I am disappointed on a tennis front, the health and well-being of my family and my team will always be my priority. Thank you to my fans for your continued support, I can't wait to play for you again."

On the upside, Ash achieved an 18-year first for Australian tennis by retaining the World No. 1 ranking through an entire year to 2021, without picking up a racquet after February.

She was as philosophical, as usual, as she prepared for the year ahead.

"All you can do is do the best every single match and that's how I'm going to approach Adelaide, that's how I'm going to approach the Australian Open and that's how I'm going to try and approach the rest of my career.

But for Ash 2020 turned out to be a lost year, playing in just four tournaments in January and February.

The start of 2020 saw a new-look tennis roster, thanks to Covid restrictions and fears; the status of the women's Brisbane International in early January, traditionally the first significant tournament of the year, appeared to be reduced with the introduction of the men's ATP Cup that was given priority scheduling on centre court and the women relegated to lesser courts.

Ash began the year shakily in Brisbane, losing her opening singles match (after a bye in the first round) to American qualifier and world No. 53 Jennifer Brady 6-4, 7-6 (7-4). Brady was later to become her doubles partner.

"You can call it rust or you can just call it a bit of execution," Ash said.

She reached the finals of the Brisbane International doubles with Dutch partner Kiki Bertens, going down 3-6, 7-6 (9-7), 10-8 in a close battle to top seeds Hsieh Su-wei and Barbora Strycova. Ash had pledged her prizemoney (about $65,000) to the Red Cross Appeal arising from recent devasting Australian bushfires.

From Brisbane it was on to Adelaide for another new event on the pro tour and another milestone achieved in her already outstanding career.

The Adelaide title was Ash's first WTA Trophy on a home

court and the first by an Australian on a home court since 2011 (Jarmila Wolfe in Hobart in 2011). Ash had been runner up twice in the Sydney International (2018 and 2019). In Adelaide, She defeated world No. 24 Ukranian Dayana Yastremska 6-2, 7-5.

"With everything that's been going on in Australia, the way that everyone's come together has been incredible and I'm bloody proud to be an Aussie," Ash said at the trophy presentation.

So it was with a high degree of confidence that she went to Melbourne for the Australian Open from 20 January.

She claimed another record there; her victory over Alison Riske in three sets saw her become the first Australian to qualify for consecutive Australian Open quarter finals since Pat Rafter 32 years earlier.

She went on to reach the semi-finals, the first Australian woman to do that since 1984, and faced American Sofia Kenin.

But the chance of taking the Australian title eluded Ash; she succumbed in straight sets, 7-6, 7-5 in an hour and 45 minutes.

It may have been the 39 degrees in the cauldron or just a case of missed opportunities, but Ash's disappointment was obvious without her having to say as much. The crowd was left stunned but eventually gave Ash a great ovation as she left the court.

She was philosophical at her press conference and referred to "perspective".

She entered the room carrying her baby niece, Olivia. "This is what life is all about. It's amazing," she said. "It's my newest niece. My sister just had her about 11, 12 weeks ago.

"I mean, perspective is a beautiful thing. Life is a beautiful thing. She brought a smile to my face as soon as I came off the court. I got to give a hug. It's all good. It's all good."

The match itself? "I think (it was) a match where I didn't feel super comfortable," Ash said. "I felt like my first plan wasn't working. I couldn't execute the way that I wanted. I tried to go to B and C. I think I had to dig and find a way. I mean, I'm two points away from winning that in straight sets, which is disappointing. Knowing I had to fight and scrap, I still gave myself a chance to win the match."

Disappointing for fans, but not so much to Ash herself. As she pointed out, she was only a point away from winning both sets in the semi-final and earning a place in the final. Instead, she lost a thrilling encounter in straight sets.

The stats told this story: Ash hit more winners and had a better winner to unforced error ratio — 33 winners and 36 unforced errors to Kenin's 15 and 26.

They each had four break point chances — Kenin converted two, Barty converted one.

Kenin had the better points record, winning 81 to Ash's 78. Sofia Kennin went on to take the Australian title, her maiden Grand Slam win, defeating Spaniard Garbine Muguruza 4-6, 6-2, 6-2.

While prizemoney seems rarely to be on her mind there was some gain to her bank account: Ash pocketed $A1,040,000 prizemoney for her semi-final result in Melbourne (and

$A38,000 for her second-round loss in the women's doubles with Julia Goerges).

The 2020 WTA Schedule was to comprise 60 events, including 55 WTA tournaments, four Grand Slams, and the Olympics.

But COVID-19 struck the world in March, resulting in five months without an event and the world rankings frozen.

By June, the WTA schedule was down to just 20 events for the rest of the year when the tour restarted in August in Italy. By then many players were not able or willing to travel because of COVID-19 requirements and restrictions. When there were tournaments, there were no crowds.

The first slam since the virus outbreak was the US Open in September. Several top players — including Ash — did not enter, the women's title going to Naomi Osaka, who then did not contest the French Open.

"It has been a difficult decision to make but unfortunately I will not be competing in Europe this year," Barty said in a statement on Instagram.

But as things turned out, without a tournament win to her name and not taking part in any late-year tournaments, she remained World No. 1 at the end of 2020 going into 2021.

A series of withdrawals and upsets from the US Open through to Paris meant she was the first Australian to end consecutive years at No. 1 since Lleyton Hewitt in 2001–2002.

Ash wasn't completely idle in the isolation from tennis for most of the year in which she turned 24. Nor did she go empty-handed for trophies and awards.

During the Australian Open she was named 2020 Young Australian of the Year, receiving the honour during the tournament. "It's a privilege, it's an honour, and extremely humbling," she said. "I'm just trying to be true to myself and stick to the values that my mum and dad taught me, that my family have kind of instilled in me growing up."

She always showed promise in golf, so it was no surprise to those who have watched her sporting career that she became the Brookwater Golf Club women's champion in 2020 while sitting out of tennis.

She claimed her club championship with a decisive seven-and-five win in the match-play final.

The break from tennis saw Ash reduce her golfing handicap from 10 to four. She played rounds during the year with tennis champion Pat Rafter and her boyfriend Garry Kissick, a PGA trainee professional at Brookwater.

Tennis stayed off her agenda until 2021. But with rankings frozen, she was still No. 1.

# 15

# 2021: LOOKING FOR 'NORMAL'

The 2021 Women's Tennis Association worldwide tour began with great optimism for a complete season.

But it was evident quite early that wouldn't be the case. Crowd numbers were being limited and some tournaments were scrubbed. Players were wary, some opting out of tournaments. COVID-19 still had the world in its grip.

The WTA cancelled the Asian swing, most significantly tournaments in Japan and China, for a second year. Only the WTA Finals in Shenzhen were left on the Asian calendar by mid-year, and it was eventually switched to Mexico.

Some other events were re-scheduled when border controls and travel amid pandemic restrictions became a problem for players and their entourages.

To make up for some of the shortfall, Melbourne hosted four extra tournaments around the Australian Open near the start of the year.

The first was the Yarra Valley Classic in January and February which saw Ash return to court after her 2020 lay-off. She dropped two sets in preliminary matches and had a walkover from Serena Williams before reaching the final where she accounted for Spaniard Garbine Muguruza 7-6, 6-4.

Ash went into the Australian Open later in February as warm favourite, but stumbled in the quarter-finals, going down 6-1, 3-6, 2-6 to Czech Karolina Muchova.

She joined American Jennifer Brady in the doubles, but they withdrew in the round of 32.

A week later Ash was in Adelaide, where she lost early to American Danielle Collins in straight sets, 3-6, 4-6.

These early results had some overseas commentators questing her worthiness to be world No. 1 as she headed for the US.

Miami had been a happy hunting ground previously and it was no surprise to see Ash battle her way through to the final, dropping three sets on the way.

She faced Bianca Andreescu of Canada in the final and took the first set 6-3. Her opponent retired in the second, with Ash leading 4-0. That gave her a second title for the year. The win also silenced some of the chatter about her holding on to the No. 1 ranking while having most of 2020 off.

Ash responded: "I never have to prove anything to anyone. I know all the work that I do with my team behind the scenes.

"I know there has been a lot of talk about the ranking, but I didn't play at all last year and I didn't improve any of my points whatsoever.

"Yes, I didn't drop, but I didn't improve any. I didn't play any at all. There were girls who had the chance to improve theirs, so I felt like I thoroughly deserve my spot at the top of the rankings."

A fair point. Those who had a chance to gain significant points on her didn't, and her lead remained intact.

Her schedule was to take her away from home for almost the rest of the year.

After Miami, it was off to Stuttgart in April. Again, she dropped three sets on the way to the final against Belarusian Aryna Sabalenka. She dropped the first set but fought back to take the match 3-6, 6-0, 6-3.

Ash triumphed in doubles, too, pairing with Jennifer Brady to win their first WTA title. They defeated top-seeded Americans Bethanie Mattek-Sands and Desirae Krawczyk 6-4, 5-7, 10-5 (modified decider format).

It was Ash's 12th career doubles title, the first since winning the Rome title with Victoria Azarenka in May 2019.

She also became the first player to scoop both the singles and doubles titles in Stuttgart since American Lindsay Davenport in 2001.

Ash wasn't quite as convincing a fortnight later in Madrid where she came up against Sabalenka again in singles, dropping the first set to love, winning the second 6-3 and losing the decider 4-6.

In Rome later in May, Ash was sound in her first two matches, not dropping a set, before having to retire when playing American Coco Gauff and leading 6-4, 2-1 in their quarter-final.

Ash's arm injury raised questions about the rest of her

schedule including the French Open and Wimbledon. She also played with strapping on her left thigh in Rome.

She didn't seem fazed, saying of the arm injury: "It's something I have had to manage over my career. It's an injury that began when I was quite young, when I was 15 or 16 years old. It just pops up every now and again," she explained.

"It became worse while we were playing. So I think that's the challenging thing, is to make the decision to stop. It's never nice. It's the thing that I hate the most is not being able to finish a tennis match. But the pain was becoming too severe, so it was important that I listen to my body and of course try and do the right thing, knowing that we have a Grand Slam in two weeks' time."

Just two years previously she had triumphed at Roland Garros in Paris and was looking forward to the chance of revisiting success there in 2021.

But injury intervened again.

Down 6-1, 2-2 against Poland's Magda Linette, Ash appeared dejected as she decided it was "unsafe" to carry on and possibly exacerbate a debilitating condition. It was her hip this time.

Her disappointment at having to withdraw in Paris was obvious, but she remained optimistic: "It's heartbreaking. I mean, we have had such a brilliant clay court season, and to kind of get a little bit unlucky with timing more than anything to have something kind of acute happen over the weekend and just kind of run out of time against the clock is disappointing. It won't take away the brilliant three months that we have had, as much as it hurts right now.

"We did everything, absolutely everything we could to give myself a chance. And, you know, it was a small miracle that we were able to get on court for that first round. Again, today it was no better and getting worse again.

"It's really disappointing. But like I said, we have had an exceptional last two, two-and-a-half, three months, a little bit of a setback, and what happened today and this week here in Paris won't take away from that. We have had a brilliant, brilliant time."

Questions were asked about whether she could even make it to Wimbledon, let alone advance through the preliminaries and on to a final.

"I've had my fair share of tears this week. It's all good. Everything happens for a reason. There will be a silver lining in this eventually," Ash said.

"Once I find out what that is, it'll make me feel a little bit better — but it will be there, I'm sure."

She had won two WTA titles, in Miami and Stuttgart, made another final in Madrid and had a run of clay-court performances that reinforced her world No. 1 status.

21

# RISING THROUGH THE RANKINGS

**2009:** (Age 13) ITF Junior Ranked 1876. Played on ITF junior circuit.

**2010:** ITF Junior Ranked 147. Played five events on WTA circuit.

**2011:** ITF Junior Ranked 2. Won girls singles at Wimbledon. WTA Ranked 679, still a junior.

**2012:** (WTA tour debut): Reached WTA No.176, second highest ranked 16-year-old in the world. Finishes year as No.195 in singles and 172 in doubles.

**2013:** Ranked 164 in singles after playing primarily on the WTA tour for the first year. Ranks No.12 in doubles.

**2014:** Ranked 218 in singles and 39 in doubles.

**2015:** (Year off) Ranked 571.

**2016:** Ranked 623 upon her return and finishes year at

No.325 in singles and 261 in doubles.

**2017:** Ranked 17 in singles and 11 in doubles.

**2018:** Ranked 15 in singles, 7 in doubles.

**MARCH 2019:** Into the Top 10, ranked No.9 in singles and doubles. When told she'd made it into the top 10: "There you go. How bloody good. It's been a goal of mine, that's no secret. And it's amazing what happens when you put your hopes and dreams out into the universe and do the work. It's amazing."

**JULY 2019:** Ash is ranked No.1 in singles. With almost seven weeks at the top, she became Australia's longest-serving women's world number one; Evonne Goolagong Cawley held the number one position for two weeks in 1976. Ash still occupied the No.1 spot at the end of Wimbledon before Naomi Osaka regained it when Ash lost to Sofia Kenin in the second round of the Toronto Masters early in August.

Ash and Victoria Azarenka lost their doubles semi-final in Toronto 6-3 3-6 4-10 (modified scoring) to top ranked Czech Republic Pair, Barbora Krejcikova and Katerina Siniakova.

Ash went into the next tournament, the Cincinnati Open, as top seed and ranked No.2 in the world. She had the No.1 ranking in her sights again when she reached the semi-finals and Naomi Osaka withdrew through injury and the other contender for No.1, Karolina Pliskova, lost in the quarter-finals to Svetlana Kuznetsova.

On the way to the semi-final Ash defeated Maria Sharapova, Anett Kontaveit and Maria Sakkari.

After advancing to the semi-final Ash was still looking to the US Open: "I think that's the beauty of being able to stay alive in the tournament, to give myself an opportunity to keep getting better. I think I'm still aiming to obviously do very well here, but the big picture is New York in ten days' time."

Svetlana Kuznetsova defeated Ash Barty in straight sets in the semi-final, temporarily denying Ash the chance to regain top spot. Kuznetsova lost narrowly to American Madeleine Keys in the final.

After the Cincinnati Open, the new WTA world rankings saw Ash at No.2 as the tour headed into the year's fourth and final grand slam at Flushing Meadows for the US Open where players would defend their rankings points from the previous year.

Ash was defending only 240 points from 2018 and was seeded No.2 while world No.1 Naomi Osaka, going in under an injury cloud, was defending 2,000 points after winning the title in 2018.

Ash at No.2 in the rankings had 6501 points, only 105 behind Naomi Osaka and 186 points ahead of Karolina Pliskova.

The draw pitted Ash against 77-ranked Zarina Diyas of Kazakhstan in the opening round. Ash won in three sets, then accounted for Lauren Davis of the US in two sets, the second in a tie-break.

Her third-round opponent was No.30 seed and good friend Maria Sakkari (Greece), who claimed a set from her the previous week in Cincinnati. Although the first set was tight, Ash prevailed in straight sets.

The win and a place in the fourth round meant a chance for Ash to return to world No.1 by year's end; Naomi Osaka who deposed her after Wimbledon needed to defend her 2018 US title and challenger Karolina Pliskova needed at least to win a semi-final.

Ash lost in straight sets to 18$^{th}$ seed Wang Qiang (China) in the fourth round, 2-6 4-6. Wang in turn was bundled out by Serena Williams who then lost the final to Canadian teenager Bianca Andreescu, missing yet another chance to equal Australian Margaret Court's record 24 grand slams titles.

Ash regained her status as WTA World No.1 when the new rankings were issued the day after the US Open finished. She had lost the No.1 spot to Naomi Osaka briefly on August 11. Despite suffering a last-16 exit at Flushing Meadows, Osaka's demise at the same stage meant the Japanese player failed to defend the points she won in taking the US title in 2018 and slipped down the rankings.

The same fate befell Pliskova, the other challenger for the No.1 spot when she also was eliminated from the US Open in the round of 16.

Ash had a good record against the top 10 players in 2019,

winning six matches. She beat then world No.1 Simona Halep at the Sydney International and followed later in the year with wins over Kiki Bertens (twice), Petra Kvitova, Karolina Pliskova and Aryna Sabalenka.

**2020–2021:** Victory in the Shenzhen finals ensured Ash finished 2019 as world No. 1. She stayed at the top through the disrupted 2020 season as tournaments were cancelled or rescheduled and rankings were frozen for much of the season. Even in tournaments that went ahead without Ash, her challengers failed to make ground and she held her ranking throughout the year and began 2021 as the one the field had to catch. Withdrawals by significant players from the "majors" left Ash at No. 1 and victory at Wimbledon meant she had spent 77 consecutive weeks as world No. 1, overtaking American Chris Evert to hold the 10th-longest streak. The win also meant Ash had spent 84 weeks in the world's top 10.

22

# 2019: THE YEAR OF SLAMS AND TITLES ON THE WAY TO NO. 1.

By reaching the fourth round of the US Open at Flushing Meadows in August 2019, Ash became the only female player to make it to the second week (fourth round) of all the year's Grand Slam tournaments.

## MELBOURNE

Ash went into the first Grand Slam of the year in Melbourne as Australia's No.1 and ranked No.15 in the WTA women's singles and No.7 in doubles.

Tennis greats John McEnroe and Martina Navratilova had said she was the best volleyer in the women's game.

She was relatively untroubled in the three early rounds, winning in straight sets over lower-ranked opponents. The fourth round proved her real test, as she came up against Maria Sharapova.

Ash prevailed in three sets 4-6 6-1 6-4 to become the first Australian woman to advance to a quarter-final at their home Grand Slam since Jelena Dokic in 2009.

The match was not without a minor controversy.

Sharapova took an unusually long bathroom break at the end of the second set that had the crowd booing her belated return.

All this didn't seem to deter Ash who finished off the match comfortably when Sharapova served a string of double faults and sprayed backhand errors around the court.

The win pitched Ash into a quarter-final against Petra Kvitova. It was a tense fight, with Kvitova receiving a time violation in the eighth game of the second set. Kvitova also became quite vocal when winning points. When asked later if it appeared Kvitova was attempting to get under her skin with her vocal second set, the 22-year-old Queenslander replied: "Not at all, not at all".

Ash lost in straight sets 1-6 4-6, but not without a good fight in the second.

## *HER PRESS CONFERENCE:*

"Disappointed purely from having competed my whole life. I'm driven to win every single match. Today Petra was outstanding, she really was. She took it away from me quite early in the match. She's very capable of doing that, I suppose.

"I've always been extremely driven and passionate, especially coming back this second time around, about how I've wanted to go about things.

"I think more importantly I've begun to understand better off the court how I can enjoy it more and enjoy the process, trust the process, get the results that we're after.

"There's nothing better than a night session at the Australian Open, particularly for it to be quarter-finals, so exciting. Even though the result didn't go my way today, I enjoyed every minute.

"Petra is absolutely capable of taking a match away from someone. I knew that going in. At times it's very much out of my control, what she does from her end of the court. In the beginning, she served particularly well. Even when I was hitting my spots on first serves, she was returning within a metre or two of the baseline, putting me on the back foot instantly.

"Yeah, she was clean as a whistle tonight. I have to give all credit to her. I wasn't nervous at all. I was excited. I don't think it was a slow start. It was more of a Petra start. She took the match away from me. It was very much out of my control. I know that I did everything possible to try and get myself back into that match. But she was too good tonight.

"I think I've done everything that I can. I finished the season of 2018 with a title. I've had my best start to 2019. Certainly, no complaints from here."

## MIAMI

Ash collected the biggest singles title of her career to that point, defeating Karolina Pliskova 7-6 (7-1 tiebreak) 6-3 to win the Miami Open in March. Pliskova was ranked seven and had defeated Simona Halep in the semi-final.

The victory put Ash into the WTA top 10, the first Australian to reach there since Sam Stosur in 2013. She also became the first Australian winner of the tournament.

Ash was 3-1 behind at one point in the first set but her fine shot-making forced a tiebreak in which she won six consecutive points to take it comfortably.

Ash served a career-high 15 aces in the final on her way to add a fourth WTA singles title to her record after the 2017 Malaysian Open and in 2018 at Nottingham and Zhuhai, China.

One of those she defeated along the way was fellow Australian Sam Stosur, Ash prevailing 6-0 6-3 in their second-round match.

## *HER PRESS CONFERENCE:*

"It's been an amazing fortnight of tennis. It really has. I think it's pretty cool to have played such a good match today, obviously in a big situation and a big match. Certainly proud of myself and happy the way that my team and I have been able to get through these two weeks.

"It was going to be a match of small opportunities. I think I was able to claw my way back into the first set and take an opportunity when I got it in the tiebreak.

"I think it was important for me to try and get that first set. I think that first set today was going to be massive. I was able to get a bit of a roll on in the second early and keep the foot down.

"It feels like it's a long time ago now since I took the break and since I came back. It's been a few years now, but I certainly feel like I'm a very different person. I feel like I'm a more complete player, I'm a better player. I have been able to put myself into more high-pressure situations and in bigger matches.

"So, it's been, you know, a helluva couple years since my comeback. I can't really complain at all. There were zero expectations. I think all it is, it's an opportunity for me to continue to try and get better every day and to enjoy the journey that we're on.

"It's been a beautiful two or three years since I have been coming back into the sport. I have been certainly able to grab my opportunities with both hands. I have had some heartbreaking losses but also some pretty amazing moments, too.

"When I can go out there and play my brand of tennis, that's when it becomes most exciting and most enjoyable for me. I'm being able to do that more and more often.

"And I think the best thing is I do feel like, you know, I belong on this tour. I feel like when I play my best, I'm good enough to match it with the very best in the world. I just need to keep giving myself the opportunity to challenge myself and play against the best in the world.

"You know, some days it will go in your favour and some days it won't. I think the challenge and the beauty is to just keep going and putting one foot in front of the other and enjoying the journey."

## FRANCE

Ash's clash in the clay court French Open final with Marketa Vondrousova of the Czech Republic was a little anticlimactic after her semi-final.

The result was an emphatic 6-1 6-3 over the Czech teenager to win her first Grand Slam in just an hour and 10 minutes. The stats:

| | Barty | Vondrousova |
|---|---|---|
| Aces | 3 | 1 |
| Double faults | 1 | 3 |
| Break points won | 5/13 | 1/4 |
| Net points won | 15/20 | 8/16 |
| Winners | 27 | 10 |
| Unforced errors | 26 | 22 |
| Total points won | 69 | 49 |

Ash showed no signs of nerves as might have been expected on such a big occasion but quickly asserted her varied skills, grabbing the first set in just 30 minutes.

Vondrousova was more competitive in the second set, forcing tougher rallies and longer games, but was unable to turn the match around.

The win took Ash to No.8 in WTA rankings, with Wimbledon now firmly on the radar.

Ash reached the final after a three-set epic semi-final battle with American teen Amanda Anisimova, eventually prevailing 6-7 (7-4 tiebreak) 6-3 6-3. The 17-year-old Anisimova beat defending champion, Simona Halep, in the quarter-finals and Ash defeated American Madison Keys in straight sets.

Anisimova took the first set from Ash in a tiebreaker, but Ash showed her spirit and determination in the second set to win six successive games and level the match.

A seven-minute game that featured four deuces on Ash's serve opened the deciding set with Anisimova getting a break to lead 2-1.

Ash hit back on her fourth break point in the fourth game to regain the momentum. In light rain she eventually closed out the victory on her sixth match point.

Some upsets helped clear Ash's path through the finals, with potential opponents Serena Williams, Naomi Osaka and Simona Halep all eliminated early. But there was no denying her status as French Open Champion, Australia's first for 46 years.

*HER PRESS CONFERENCE:*

"For a lot of the Aussies out there, I think for us it's a celebration of not just these two weeks but the last two or three years for myself and my team. I have an extraordinary group of genuine, authentic people around me.

"This is just a by-product of what we've been able to do, all the work that we have done, and it's incredible and I'm speechless.

"At the moment it's a bit too much and a bit out there, really. But it's amazing. I mean, we have done the work, and we tried to put ourselves in these positions. Now that we're here, it's just incredible.

"Oh, it's been an incredible couple of weeks, that's for sure. I think any time I can play my brand of tennis I can match it against the best in the world.

"For the last fortnight, the stars have aligned for me. I have been able to play really good tennis when I've needed it.

"This is just incredible. I never dreamt that I'd be sitting here with this trophy at the French Open. I mean, obviously we have dreams and goals as children, but this is incredible.

"I think probably that match in Rome was the only match of the whole year that I felt like I walked off the court and I was a little bit disappointed with how I played and how I was out there.

"But it was a very quick and easy turnaround. I think having doubles certainly helped and playing those few extra matches with Vika was unreal, and I felt like I was striking the ball well. Then it was about managing my body and making sure that I was as fit as possible to come here and enjoy it and play well.

"Yeah, I think I played well last year on the clay. I'm learning more and more every single time that I play, learning how to use my variety and use it as best I can. It's just been an amazing two weeks.

"Yesterday was an absolute roller coaster. There's no way to think about it. I think I played some really good tennis and some pretty awful tennis. Then today I just kept saying to myself, I may never get this opportunity ever again, so try and grab it with both hands.

"I felt like for me it was the perfect tennis match, considering the situation, the conditions, and kind of all of the above. It was amazing.

It's been a natural progression of, you know, becoming stronger, not growing any taller, but getting stronger and being able to trust myself and hit my spots on my serve.

"My serve is a massive part of my game, and I try and think my way around the court. I know where opponents like to return, and if they shift their position, where they return and I try and expose those spots as best that I can. I don't even know if I'd be sitting here talking to you if I was playing tennis if I didn't step away.

"It's obviously a part of my life that I needed to deal with, and I feel like it was the best decision that I made at the time, and it was an even better one coming back."

## BIRMINGHAM

Ash Barty was pitted against doubles one-time partner and close friend world number 19 Julia Goerges of Germany in the Birmingham final at the Edgbaston Priory Club on 8 July.

The German posed a serious threat in the second set when she led 3-0. But Ash showed her resolve by hitting back to take out the match in just under 90 minutes, 6-3 7-5.

On the way to the final and subsequently the World No.1 ranking, Ash defeated Donna Vekic (Croatia), Jennifer Brady (USA), Venus Williams (USA) and Barbora Strycova (Czech Republic).

Naomi Osaka of Japan had the chance to hold on to the top ranking if she could have progressed to the quarter-finals and beyond, but she lost in the second round.

The Birmingham Classic was Ash's 11th successive victory and to then her most recent defeat was on 16 May against Kristina Mladenovic at the Italian Open in Rome.

*HER PRESS CONFERENCE:*

"Jules is an incredible competitor and she is never going to hand a match over lightly and she is always going to come up with her best stuff when her back is against the wall. So it was important for me to try and stay in touch and getting that break back early in the set was really important to not kind of give her a sniff of winning a set on her serve.

"We've got to this point by doing all the small things right and I think we will continue to try and do that. But it's certainly just been the most amazing month of tennis for us and really an amazing three years.

"It is always a goal to try and be the best. It's ultimately why we train, why we compete and play, but for it to happen in this way has been amazing. It's a testament to all of my team who have put so much time and invested so much passion and energy into my career and try and make me the best that I can be.

"It's just hard to put into words what we have been able to achieve over the last few years and to be where we are now is just incredible. Obviously Jules and I are very close and it is tough whenever you are playing a friend, but I know that I respect her and she respects me enough to be put that aside while we are on the court.

"But then as soon as we shake hands, no matter who has won or lost the match, the relationship doesn't change and it's a testament to Jules as a character, she is an incredible person, someone I highly respect and love to spend time with. And yeah, I couldn't think of a better person to be able to share the court with today.

We have always enjoyed practicing together and spending time with each other and as I said it's hard playing a friend but in a final I think you'd love to play a friend knowing you have both earnt that spot.

"I think I have to trust myself and trust that I can execute on those big points, and not just when I'm set-point down but also on those crucial 30-All, 15-30 points. But at the end of the day, there's no point that means anything more than the next one, they all have the same value, so it is about trying to execute as best as I can on that point and if it's at 15-Love, or set-point down, it doesn't change for me."

Ash became only the fifth Australian to be crowned World No.1 and only the second Australian female to hold the ranking after Evonne Goolagong Cawley in 1976.

The WTA rankings were introduced in 1975. Rankings were calculated fortnightly until 1990, and a search of the records many years later revealed that Evonne overtook Chris Evert by 0.8 of a ranking point after the Australian's victory in the Virginia Slims Championships in Los Angeles in late April, before Evert regained the crown on 10 May.

Ash didn't see herself in the same league as Evonne, even though she would hold the No.1 ranking for longer.

In her words: "I'm nowhere near her status. To be mentioned in the same sentence is incredible. Evonne, she's an amazing human being and has set the tone for so many Australians and so many indigenous Australians around our country and around the world. She is an amazing person. And what she has done in her career was incredible and what she continues to do off the court for us as a sport is amazing."

## WIMBLEDON

Ash headed into the world's most famous tennis championship on 2 July as the top seed, favourite and highest-ranked female player in the game.

Her first-round opponent was world No.43 Saisai Zheng of China, Ash prevailing 6-4 6-2. In her part of the draw sat two-time Grand Slam champions, Svetlana Kuznetsova and Garbine Muguruza, with Serena Williams and triple major champion Angelique Kerber as possible opponents if she made the quarter-finals.

The second round saw her defeat Alison Van Uytvanck of Belgium 6-1 6-3. That took her to the fourth round where she posted a convincing straight-sets defeat of Briton Harriet Dart 6-1 6-1 in 53 minutes on Centre Court, to book her place in the last 16 against 55th-ranked American Alison Riske.

The win over Dart extended her winning streak to 15 matches, the last 10 without dropping a set.

Riske was a formidable opponent, despite her ranking and Ash went down in three sets, 6-3 2-6 3-6, denied a possible semi-finals clash with Serina Williams. Her loss to the American was Ash's first in 16 matches and only her seventh in nine months.

Ash opened with four straight aces and seemed in control as she took the first set. Power shots by Riske and some unforced errors from Ash turned the game in the American's favour and she won the last two sets without much trouble as Ash's first serve dominance deserted her.

In her words: "I started really well, was able to hit my spots. In the second set, I gave Alison too many looks at second serves. I know that my percentage was down. I wasn't missing serves by too much. They were small margins. A miss is still a miss and gives her an opportunity to have a look at a second serve."

Riske was beaten in the semi-finals by Serena Williams who was yet again denied the chance to equal Australian Margaret Court's Grand Slam win record of 24 when she lost in straight sets in the final, giving Romanian Simona Halep her first Grand Slam victory.

After winning at Birmingham, Ash withdrew from the next lead-up tournament, at Eastbourne, saying she wanted to rest her arm where an old injury had flared. She downplayed any effect that had on her Wimbledon results.

She also withdrew from the Wimbledon women's doubles and declined an invitation to play with Brit Andy Murray in the mixed championship.

## *HER PRESS CONFERENCE:*

"I lost to a better player. Absolutely no regrets. We've planned our days and prepared as best that we can. Today wasn't my day. I think I started well. I was sticking to how I wanted to play. Then in the second set, I think my serve let me down. I let

Alison get back into the match too many times, having looks at second serves.

"Overall I didn't play a poor match. When I needed to, when the big moments were there, Alison played better today. Tough one to swallow but I lost to a better player.

"I'm so proud of myself and my team over the last six to eight weeks. We've had an incredible trip, incredible couple of months.

"If that's the case, it won't really change what we do. We'll go home, rest a little bit, then head down again, work hard, and head over to the States.

"You just have to look at her (Alison's) stats on a grass court to show just how dangerous she is. She's very comfortable on the grass court. It complements her game well. I think today in the crunch moments, she came up with her best tennis. When her back is against the wall, she plays really well typically. She did that today. All credit to her.

"She deserves to be in the quarter-finals. She played a great match today.

"Overall it's been a hell of a trip. Disappointed right now. Obviously it's a tough pill to swallow. In the same breath, it's been an incredible few months. New ground for me here at Wimbledon. This is the best we've done.

"Yeah, very proud of what we've been able to achieve. Today wasn't my day. I didn't win a tennis match. It's not the end of the world. It's a game. I love playing the game. I do everything in my power to try and win every single tennis match. But that's not the case.

"Today, it's disappointing right now. Give me an hour or so, we'll be all good. The sun's still going to come up tomorrow (smiling)."

## THE NEXT ASSIGNMENT

The American spring usually comprises seven ATP World Tour and WTA events beginning in Atlanta and culminating in the final Grand Slam of the year in August, the US Open at Flushing Meadows where the field would comprise 13 Grand Slam women's singles champions, including the newest, Ash Barty.

In her words: "In the US, which I love that time of year, I love getting back over to the summertime there. I have some really good memories from last year. We go back, we knuckle down, train again, then we go again."

Ash's exit from Wimbledon had no effect on her No.1 ranking, her best-ever finish at the grass court Grand Slam gave her a lead of 348 points on Japan's Naomi Osaka (6605 to 6257).

Karolina Pliskova remained at No.3. Wimbledon champion Simona Halep moved up three places to No.4 and Serina Williams moved up one place to No.9.

With the North American leg of the WTA tour starting in Montreal on 5 August, it remained possible Ash could still be No.1 at the end of the year.

## US OPEN

Ash rebounded from a poor start to defeat Zarina Diyas of Kazakhstan 1-6 6-3 6-2 in the first round of the US Open, in one hour and 41 minutes.

Ash had previously played Diyas once, also a tight contest, for a 7-6 (tiebreaker) 6-4 win in the second round of the Kuala Lumpur tournament in 2013.

For the first half hour, Ash struggled to find her range on serve and groundstrokes. She was just a set away from a shock upset but gradually took control as her serves started to find their mark.

In her words: "I just didn't give myself a chance in that first set, sort of appalling, probably made a set's worth of errors. We were able to find a way after that to get into the match and be more patient and really just lock down and wait until I got the right balls and right patterns that I wanted. That was probably the biggest change in the second and third — I was able to get more of those patterns more regularly and in the end build pressure to create more opportunities to break."

Ash was pushed hard by No.73 ranked American Lauren Davis in the second round in a match switched to indoors after rain delays. She won the first set comfortably but had to fight back from a break down before overcoming a set point in a long 12th game to earn a 6-2 7-6 (7/2) victory in just more than two hours.

The win took Ash's grand slam record to 16-2 in 2019 as she homed in on her result in the US Open from last year when she reached the fourth round.

In her words: "I knew I was doing the right thing; it was just a bit about execution, It was difficult conditions out there. But I'm very happy to come through and play a really good tie breaker."

Her third-round match against No.30 seed Maria Sakkari of Greece in Louis Armstrong Stadium saw Ash set up a fourth-round appearance for the second successive time at a US Open. Ash won 7-5 6-3, dropping serve only once and breaking her opponent four times.

Ash first appeared in a fourth round of a Grand Slam tournament at the US Open in 2018, losing to Karolina Pliskova. Sakkari beat Ash at Indian Wells in 2018.

The match became a battle between Ash's dangerous slice and her opponent's heavy topspin.

Her slices to Sakkari's forehand drew mistakes with Sakkari making 25 unforced errors to only seven winners in the first set.

Ash's serve also proved a factor, posting five aces to Sakkari's none. Breaks were exchanged but Ash took the final two games from 5-5 to grab the first set.

Ash increased her first serve percentage from 41% to 54% in the second set, adding a further six aces. Sakkari wilted, making four successive unforced errors to take her total for the match to 38, and giving Ash victory and giving her a chance to reach her third major quarter-final for the year. A clash with Serena Williams was possible.

In her words: "Maria is an incredible competitor, a great mover around the court and plays her best tennis when she's on the move and so it was important for me to try and dictate without going into her patterns. It's tricky to play a friend but I was really happy with the way I able to close out those two sets."

An uncharacteristic 39 unforced errors saw Ash bow out in the fourth round to 18th seed Wang Qiang, of China, in straight sets 2-6 4-6.

From 2015 until earlier in 2019, Wang was coached by Australian three-time Grand Slam doubles champion Peter McNamara, who died of cancer in July.

Ash had nine break points but could not convert any of them. In her words: "I felt like she was able to put the ball with great depth in difficult positions for me. I still was able to create opportunities, it was just very frustrating that on the big points today, she played a lot better. I had nine break points, and I wasn't able to even get one of them, which is really frustrating. I don't think the second week of a Slam is a missed opportunity. It's a hell of an effort for all Slams to get to the second week. Yes, I would have loved to have done better. It wasn't to be. But certainly not something I'm stressed about. Obviously I would have loved to have kept going here in singles, but we've got an opportunity to do that in doubles."

The loss made her win/loss record for the year 45-9, and 229-87 for her career. Ash's fourth-round loss raised questions from some commentators about the wisdom of her doubles commitments, particularly as between her third and fourth round clashes she and partner Victoria Azarenka played a match that lasted more than two hours.

The pair continued to shine in the doubles, going all the way to the final.

Ash dismissed the questions.

In her words: "There are a lot of experts out in the world. There are a lot of people who think they know my team and my body and my decision and my thinking. But, at the end of the day, it's my career and I certainly don't really take notice of that. They're not people I'm worried about. I'm here enjoying my time playing singles and doubles — I don't do it every week — but the weeks that we do, I think we certainly make the most of it."

Despite dominating for most of the match Ash and Azarenka could not convert their strengths into victory, going down 5-7 5-7 to third seeds Aryna Sabalenka (Belarus) and Elise Mertens (Belgium).

Ash and Azarenka gave up a 3-1 lead in the first set and then twice dropped serve from 40-15 up in the second.

They were unable to convert any of four break points after Mertens was trailing love-40 on serve at 3-4 in the eighth game of the second set.

In her words: "They're the what-ifs that we can't worry

about and can't stress about. I think we still have to celebrate the fact that we've had a hell of a tournament... I feel like I'm in a great place off the court and enjoying myself on the court."

## FED CUP

Ash had an impressive record in the Fed Cup (the women's international team tournament known as the Federation Cup from 1963 to 1995), winning 17 matches of the 19 she played leading up to the 2019 final, with a win/loss record of 10-1 in singles and 7-1 in doubles. She won all her all six rubbers in 2019.

She became the first Australian player to receive the International Tennis Federation's Fed Cup Heart Award.

Initiated by the ITF in 2009, the Fed Cup Heart Award recognises players who have represented their country with distinction, shown exceptional courage on court and demonstrated outstanding commitment to their team during Fed Cup matches.

Ash was nominated for the Award after leading Australia to a 3-2 victory over Belarus in the World Group semi-finals in Brisbane in April 2019. She won both her singles matches, against Aryna Sabalenka and Victoria Azarenka, and teamed with Sam Stosur to win the deciding doubles rubber, to take Australia to their first Fed Cup final in 26 years where they would face France in Perth in November (France and Australia were ranked third and fourth respectively in the 2019 Fed Cup).

Ash's award included a $US10,000 ($A14,426) grant for

the charity of her choice, the RSPCA.

Ash also became the first player to both play and win every possible match on the way to the final.

In her words: "Playing for my country is always a privilege and Fed Cup weeks are my favourite time of the year. I'm honoured to have won the Fed Cup Heart Award for my role in our semi-final win. I'm looking forward to donating the $10,000 to my charity partner, the RSPCA. Animal welfare is close to my heart and I'm happy to help provide some extra support for the wonderful work the RSPCA do. Having the chance to play in Fed Cup Final is something I have always dreamt of and I'm so happy we'll be playing the final at home in Australia. It will be another great opportunity to pull on the green and gold and work together with Alicia (Molik)."

Ash was 16 when she made her debut in the Federation Cup in 2013 and she didn't let Australia down. She was a consistent performer in a team that struggled.

By 2017, Australia faced relegation to the regional zone of the competition. Ash was pitched into the hot seat and led Australia to victory over Serbia in Zrenjanin.

Over the next two years, Australia was unbeaten. Ash became the first in the competition to contribute to every point (match win) when a team reached the final. She beat Americans Madison Keys and Sofia Kenin, then Victoria Azarenka and Aryna Sabalenka of Belarus. That took Australia to the final, in Perth, against France.

Ash won a 15th successive rubber to give Australia an early

lead. But she lost her second singles game in a two-and-a-half-hour marathon, before losing the deciding doubles match with Sam Stosur.

Kristina Mladenovic and Caroline Garcia were too good for Ash and Sam Stosur in the doubles decider, winning 6-4, 6-3 to give France a third Fed Cup.

And so Australia's bid to end a 45-year Fed Cup drought in 2019 ended in tears, literally.

There were few people more disappointed in the loss to France, 3-2, than Ash whose disappointment was clear.

But as the tears cleared, Ash said: "Even though it's bloody tough now, in a couple of days' time I think we'll be all right."

23

# ASH'S COACHES

Ash started working with her long-time junior coach Jim Joyce at the West Brisbane Tennis Centre at the age of four. Joyce did not typically train children as young as Ash but took her on because of her "excellent hand-eye coordination and high level of focus". He recalled the first session: "The first ball I threw to her, bang! She hit it right back."

Ash also practised at home: "I used to hit the ball against the wall exterior to our living room every day after school, for hours on end."

By the time she was nine, she was practising against boys six years older than her. At 12, she was competing against male adults. Former Australian tennis professional Scott Draper worked with Ash at the National Academy.

Jason Stoltenberg, who played professional tennis for 14 years and was once ranked 19 in the world, was brought in to help Ash when she was 15, just before the 2011 Wimbledon Juniors where she won the title.

"The win doesn't guarantee anything," said Stoltenberg, at the time, "but it tells you this girl is quite unique and has the ability to do things that you don't often expect."

Returning from England, she moved to Melbourne to continue training. Aged 16, she lived alone in a flat in South Yarra, doing her own laundry and cooking, using recipe notes written by her mother — including instructions on how to make a chicken wrap.

A year later she felt the pressure and loneliness. During a training session she told Stoltenberg she didn't think she could go on. "I was in tears, in his arms, and just said I couldn't do it anymore," she recalled.

So the break was made.

When she left tennis in 2014, she had amassed $A333,950 in prizemoney in the first nine months of the year. Her career earnings had reached $A1.14 million. She did not retain financial assistance from Tennis Australia as she sat out of the game.

Tennis Australia boss Craig Tiley explained: "Funding by TA for players is not direct money — it's funding for coaching, sports science services, practice and training facilities," Tiley said.

"Because she is not playing now she is not getting that funding. We are continuing to provide counselling and psych services, as we would for any of our athletes which they can access.

"It would be completely on her terms if she wants to come back. Ash is a great tennis player and is from a great family."

During her sabbatical from tennis in 2015 she didn't forsake tennis altogether, maintaining contact with Jim Joyce after she moved back north to Queensland and picking up the racket from time to time. She also helped Joyce coach children.

When she warmed to playing tennis again early in 2016, Melbourne-based Craig Tyzzer began working with her full-time. He previously coached Australian Andrew Ilie (1997-2004) to a career-high No.38 ranking.

Tyzzer played on the ATP Tour from 1979 to 1983. He worked as assistant Coach to Tony Roche and Team Manager of the Operation Tennis Elite Squad Players that included Todd Woodbridge, Richard Fromberg and Mark Kratzmann. From 1986 to 1988 he was Assistant Director of Competitive Edge (International Tennis Academy) at John Newcombe's Tennis Ranch, Texas, USA.

Tyzzer has guided Ash in her rise to No.1.

His said of work with Ash: "Most of the general public only see players when they play matches and don't realise the amount of preparation that has gone into just getting them out on court. On a general day before a tournament starts Ash could do anywhere from three-to-four hours of work to get ready. It could involve any or all of these aspects — conditioning, strength training, rehabilitation, body management, physiotherapy and massage — and that is before we even step on the court."

24

# YEAR BY YEAR

**1996:** Ashleigh Barty is born in Ipswich, Queensland. She has older sisters, Sara and Ali. Parents are Josie and Robert Barty. The family live in Springfield, a suburb of Ipswich. Ashleigh attends Woodcrest State College. Robert Barty is a Ngarigo Indigenous Australian through a grandmother. He works as a public servant. Josie works as a radiographer.

**2001:** Ashleigh, aged 5, works with junior tennis coach Jim Joyce at the West Brisbane Tennis Centre.

In her words: "I was very fortunate to have a coach when I was young who taught me all the traditional shots and taught me a pretty traditional game style."

**2009:** Ash starts playing in low-level events on the ITF Junior Circuit at the age of 13 and won her first title at the Grade 4 Australian International before turning 14.

**2010:** Ash begins her professional tennis career at an International Tennis Federation (ITF) $25,000 tournament in her hometown, Ipswich, near Brisbane. She loses her first match to Karolina Wlodarczak. Her second appearance in a main draw that year is in an ITF event in Mount Gambier where she scores her first professional win, defeating Indonesian player Ayu-Fani Damayanti 6-7 6-3 6-3.

She goes on to defeat Australian Arina Rodinova 0-6 6-2, 6-4 in the round of 16, and another Australian Sophie Letcher 7-6 6-4 in the quarter-finals. She loses to Brazilian Anna-Clara Duarte 2-6 3-6 in the semi-finals. She finishes the year with a 4-4 win/loss record.

**2011:** She plays her first junior Grand Slam event in 2011, aged 14, at the Australian Open, where she loses her opening match to third seed American Lauren Davis 0-6 3-6.

She enters three more $25,000 events in Australia; her best results are two lower tier quarter-finals appearances.

She goes on to win singles and doubles events at two high-level Grade 1 events, the Sarawak Chief Minister's Cup in Malaysia in March and the Belgian International Junior Championships in May.

After a second-round loss in the French Open Ash goes to Wimbledon and collects the Junior Wimbledon girls' crown, defeating Irina Khromacheva of Russia in the final and rising to No.2 in the ITF world junior rankings by December. Her win/loss record for the year is 13/4.

**2012:** Ash enters the main draw of a Grand Slam event for the first time in her career, the 2012 Australian Open, after winning the Wildcard Play-off with a straight-sets 7-6 6-2 victory over second seed Olivia Rogowska at the end of 2011. She doesn't drop a set in the play-offs.

She continues on the ITF Australian circuit, scoring her first win for the year in March in her first-round encounter with Australian Ashley Keir 6-0 6-0 in Ipswich, Queensland, her hometown. She wins two more matches in that tournament before losing to Polish player Sandra Zaniewska 7-8 8-1.

She goes into the main draw of the French Open in May, losing 1-6 2-6 to Petra Kvitova in the first round.

In June she returns to the ITF circuit, in Nottingham, and wins four matches (including three three-setters) on the way to the final and a straight-sets 6-1 6-1 victory over German Tatjana Marie.

Ash suffered a first-round loss at Wimbledon and returned to the ITF circuit in Australia in the latter part of 2012 with some good results, including a win in Traralgon over fellow Australian Arina Rodionov, who managed to turn the tables on Ash at Bendigo.

In her words: "I've always wanted to be my own player from the start and do things a bit differently to what the others do. I want to play my own way."

December: Ash makes her debut in the Hopman Cup team in Perth over the New Year, replacing injured Casey

Dellacqua to partner Bernard Tomic. Her WTA ranking is 175. Her win/loss record for the year is 38/11.

**2013:** Ash begins the year in the Hopman Cup and posts two wins, over Andrea Petkovic of Germany and Francesca Schiavone of Italy but loses to Ana Ivanovic of Serbia.

Ash has success in doubles on the WTA Tour, finishing runner-up at three Grand Slam doubles events with Casey Dellacqua — the Australian Open, Wimbledon and the US Open. She wins a rubber at the Federation Cup and earns a career high singles ranking of 129.

Barty and Dellacqua become the first Australian pair to reach an Australian Open women's doubles final since Evonne Goolagong and Helen Gourlay in 1977, helping Ash gain around 100 places in the world rankings.

The pair go on to Wimbledon and the US Open where they defeat three of the top 10 seeds at both events.

They collect one title for the year, the Birmingham Classic, defeating Cara Black (Zimbabwe)and Marina Erakovic (New Zealand) in the final.

Ash reaches two other tour-level semi-finals, partnering Anastasia Rodionova, and finishes the season ranked world No.12 in doubles. Her singles win/loss record is 13/13.

**2014:** Ash has a lack of significant success in singles in 2014 but has another good year in doubles with Casey Dellacqua.

They win their second title at the Internationaux de Strasbourg during the clay season and reach the quarter-finals at the French Open and Wimbledon.

They cannot repeat their title victory at the Birmingham Classic after reaching the final for the second year in a row.

In September 2014, a month after her first-round loss at the US Open, Ash announces she is taking an indefinite break from tennis.

She is ranked outside the top 200 in singles and No.40 in doubles at the time. Her win/loss record for the year is 23/11. Fishing was next on the agenda, but she found cricket might offer her a more comfortable team environment than travelling away from home most of the time to play tennis.

In her words: "It was all just too much. I was younger than the other girls on tour, so I knew them but not well. I just felt lonely and strange.

"I just wanted to come home and spend time with my family. I started playing when I was five years old. I didn't want to be driven away from the sport, so I needed to step back. I needed to enjoy just being a kid again.

"I was still enjoying life. I had nothing to complain about, I wanted to make sure I was all in or there's no point doing it. It is tough when you're by yourself and I think that's why team sport is so appealing. I'm still connected very much to tennis and everything it has to offer. It's been a part of me since I was four years old and is never going to leave me.

**2015:** Ash meets members of the Australian women's cricket team to talk about her experiences as a professional athlete. She decides to try cricket. She plays for the Western Suburbs team in the Brisbane-based Women's Premier Cricket Twenty20 league.

In her words: "I never had a dream of being number one in the world. I played tennis because I loved it and I just happened to be good at it. I'm not one for the spotlight and, you know, lots of times I just wanted to be a normal teenage girl."

Ash signs on with the Brisbane Heat in the inaugural year of the Women's Big Bash League T20 cricket competition and the Queensland Fire in the national competition.

**2016:** In February Ash returns to tennis in ITF events at the end of the WBBL season, mostly playing doubles with Jessica Moore, winning three of five tournaments.

In her words: "This time I view tennis very differently, I'm much more mature. Instead of a fifteen-year-old girl caught in the headlights, I feel like I belong now. I just can't wait to get started. Cricket and tennis are very different skill sets, but I've played tennis all my life, so it's a lot easier coming back than learning how to face a cricket ball for the first time."

Craig Tyzzer becomes her coach as she turns to singles in May and enters the second tier ITF $50,000 Eastbourne event. She is still a member of the WTA tour by way of her doubles record which earns her the entry at Eastbourne. A place opens up in the main draw through the qualifiers of which she wins three. She goes on to win three matches in the main draw to reach the quarter-finals and leaves ranked No.623.

Another run from qualifying to the quarter-finals the following week in Nottingham sees Ash cut her ranking dramatically to No.335. She makes it to the second round of Wimbledon qualifying.

After a bone stress injury in her arm, she only plays in one more event that year, the Taipei Challenger in November, again entering via qualifiers before succumbing to her injury. Her win/loss record is 16/4.

**2017:** This proves to be the real launch year for her trip to the top of the rankings; she starts the year at No.232 and finishes at a then career-high No.17.

In her words: "I certainly fear no one, and I know I can go out there and match up with the world's best."

She wins her first WTA singles title, in Malaysia, entering the top 100 for the first time, and reaches finals in two others, semi-finals in four. Her scalps include higher ranked players Venus Williams, Garbine Muguruza, Karolina Pliskova, Johanna Konta, Jelena Ostapenko, Agnieszka Radwanska and Angelique Kerber. She plays in 17 WTA events with a 42-16 win-loss record.

She collects $US1,045,826 in singles prizemoney and $US374,231 in doubles for a total of $US1,420,057 ($A1,849,614). Ash caps off the year by winning the

Newcombe Medal in the Australian Tennis Awards. Her coach Craig Tyzzer wins the award for Coaching Excellence (High Performance). Her win/loss record is 42/16.

In her acceptance speech after receiving the John Newcombe medal, Ash paid tribute to Fed Cup teammate and close friend Casey Dellacqua.

In her words: "Case, my best mate. She's not here tonight, but I don't think she quite understands how much of a massive impact she has had in my life, bringing me back into the sport to be honest. She was the one who started the ball rolling again, to sort of finish that unfinished business in doubles and now we've been able to have a pretty amazing singles and doubles year. Case is my best friend, my mum on tour, my shoulder to cry on through many times and she helped me through my darkest days and has been able to share this year with me and really helped through it the most. Case is probably the biggest thank you of all."

**2018:** After a first-round loss in the year-opener in Brisbane on New Year's Day, Ash's good form revives. She goes all the way to the final in Sydney, losing narrowly 4-6 4-6 to Angelique Kerber of Germany. After two good early wins she bows out of the Australian Open in Melbourne to Naomi Osaka in the third round 4-6 2-6. Osaka goes on to take the title and No.1 ranking on the WTA tour. Ash wins both her singles matches in the Federation Cup match against Ukraine and again in the following round against Netherlands. She bows out of Indian Wells in March in the first round, losing 4-6 2-6 to Maria Sakkari of Greece. Ash was ranked 16 at that time.

She makes it through to later rounds in Spain and France (Strasbourg). In Rome, she loses in the first round to Russian Maria Sharapova in a tight three-setter 5-7 6-3 2-6.

The French Open sees Ash get through the first round comfortably but she falls to former No.1 Serena Williams in the second round in another tight three-setter after winning the first, 6-3 and losing the next 3-6 4-6. She finishes the year as one of just two players in the Top 20 in both singles and doubles.

In her words: "Any time you get to play a champion like Serena, it's amazing. I mean, I played well. I feel like I wasn't really (doing) too much wrong. I was looking after my service games pretty well. And then I think early in the second set, in that game, at 1-0, [Serena] stepped it up a notch. You can't give someone of Serena's calibre that many looks at second serves and put yourself under the pump that much. I think there were only really a couple of games, a couple of my service games, but I don't think there was really a hell of a lot in that match."

In the lead-up to Wimbledon she loses in the second round at Birmingham to Julia Goerges and in the third round at Eastbourne to Caroline Wozniacki of Denmark. Both losses are close.

She accounts for Stefanie Voegele of Switzerland 7-5 6-3 in the first round, Canadian Eugenie Bouchard 6-4 7-5 in the second before losing in the third round to the improving Russian, Daria Kasatkina 5-7 3-6.

Montreal in August sees Ash go deep into the tournament with her victims including Kiki Bertens and Alize Cornet in straight sets before falling to Simona Halep 4-6 1-6 in the semi-finals. Halep goes on to win the tournament.

Ash makes it through to the fourth round of the US Open where she loses to Karolina Pliskova 4-6 4-6. Pliskova then loses to Serena Williams who goes on to take the title.

After a second-round loss to Victoria Azarenka in Tokyo, yet another narrow loss follows in Wuhan, China, going down to Aryna Sabalenka (Czech Republic) 6-7 4-6 in the semi-finals.

To finish the year, Ash contests the 12-player WTA Elite Trophy play-offs in Zhuhai, China. The field comprises the players ranked 9 to 20 for the year who didn't make the top 8 in the major play-offs in Singapore. Ash finished the year ranked No.15.

In an interview before the Zhuhai play-offs WTA chief executive Steve Simon said, prophetically: "If any of the players in Zhuhai this week were to make it to next year's 'Elite 8' it wouldn't be a surprise, and given the depth on display on the WTA the past two seasons, it's within the realm of possibility that one, or more, of them could be crowned a Grand Slam champion in 2019."

The 12 players were Ash, Daria Kasatkina, Elise Mertens, Aryna Sabalenka, Qiang Wang (China), Anett Kotaveit, Garbine Muguruza, Shaui Zhang (China) Madikson Keys,

Caroline Garcia (France), Anastasija Sevastova (Latvia) and Julia Görges. Ash was drawn in Group C with Sabalenka and Garcia — each player had a win, Ash defeating Garcia and moving on to the semi-finals.

Ash had a three-sets win over Goerges 4-6 6-3 6-2 in the semi-final and defeated Wang in straight sets 6-3 6-4 to claim the hardcourt title and finish 2018 on a high looking to 2019 with increased confidence after a 46/19 win/loss record and consolidating her top 20 ranking.

In her words: "There's still leaps and bounds to improve on. We're sitting at a career high of 15 and there's so much more that we can do to improve my game and continue to develop my game. Something that I was taught by my first coach when I was a lot younger is that you have to have all the shots and we're just trying to chip away at that to try and get towards a complete player.

"Generally, I'm not the biggest girl so a lot has to do with being able to hold my position on the baseline and hang with the bigger girls who can hit a bigger ball than me. Not giving them court position. Staying up in the court so I can control the points as much as possible because it isn't my game to be running side to side for two and a half hours. I like to be in control. I like to use my variety. It's no secret that I try to set up my game around my serve and my forehand and the more I do that in a match usually it's a better outcome. It's trying to put the ball in a position where I can control the point."

25

# 2019: ASCENSION TO No.1

Japan's Naomi Osaka reigned as World No.1 in women's tennis after her Australian Open victory in January 2019.

But she struggled from there on. She failed to defend her title at Indian Wells, suffered an early loss at the 2019 Miami Open before reaching her first clay court semi-final at the Stuttgart Open, where she withdrew before the match due to an abdominal injury.

At the Madrid Open, she lost a quarter-final then had to withdraw from her Italian Open quarter-final match with a hand injury. But she was still No.1.

By the French Open, the time was right for someone to step up, especially after Osaka lost in the third round. The Australian was about to seize the day. The grass of Birmingham was to be the clincher.

The WTA rankings formula is based on a rolling 52-week cumulative system, reviewed after each tournament. A player's ranking is determined by her results at a maximum of 16 tournaments for singles and 11 for doubles. Points are awarded based on how far a player advances in a tournament and the class of tournament. A player must defend any points won at the same tournament the previous year, or lose the difference from their current points. The system was modified for the 2020–2021 series and largely restored for 2022.

Ash began 2019 slowly as she set out on a quest that ultimately would take her to World No.1.

She opened up by playing singles for Australia in the Hopman Cup in Perth that began in December 2018 and finished in January 2019. It was the final Hopman Cup tournament with changes made for 2019-2020 in the Australian program. Ash won her singles match and teamed with Matthew Ebden to defeat France 2-1 by taking the doubles.

Then it was back to Sydney for her Australian season opener.

Her scalps at the Sydney International included three top 15 players, including Simona Halep for her first career victory over a reigning world No.1 player. Halep went on to claim the Wimbledon women's singles title later in the year, defeating Serena Williams in straight sets.

Home territory seemed to suit, and Ash dropped only one set in moving through to the Sydney final where she was to meet her nemesis in their previous clashes, Petra Kvitova. Kvitova had beaten Ash in their three encounters since their first meeting in 2012. The final saw a similar outcome, Kvitova just proving too strong in an extremely tight three-set contest this time.

In her words: "I'm a different player than I was 12 months ago. I feel like I'm a much better player. I'm a more complete player. You know, certainly with a week like this, I have had probably one of the best weeks of my career. You know, I feel like

I'm playing great tennis. Yes, it's a bitter pill to swallow tonight, but we move on, we keep working, and we have a Slam to look forward to in a couple of days time."

Then it was on to Melbourne for the Australian Open and again Ash was to come up against Kvitova, in the quarter-finals where Kvitova posted a seemingly comfortable two sets win. Ash was the first Australian to make the quarter-finals at the event since Jelena Dokic in 2009.

When the WTA tour arrived in Miami in March, Ash had the chance to extract revenge on Kvitova.

The Miami Masters featured many big names of women's tennis. Ash, seeded 12, claimed the scalps of compatriot Sam Stosur and Kiki Bertens from The Netherlands on the way to meeting Kvitova, seeded three, in the quarter-finals. Ash took the first set 7-6 in a tiebreaker, lost the second 2-6 but regained her composure to win the decider 6-2.

She had a two-sets win over 21-seed Anett Kontaveit of Estonia in the semi-finals to challenge number five seed and World No.7 Karolina Pliskova of the Czech Republic in the final.

Down 3-1 down in the first set, Ash fought back to beat Pliskova in straight sets 7-6 (7-1) 6-3, the biggest singles title won by an Australian player, male or female, since Sam Stosur won the US Open in 2011.

Ash previously had won tournaments in Malaysia, Nottingham and Zhuhai. Miami was her first in a WTA Premier Mandatory event.

It was Ash's eighth tournament win as a professional, the $US9 million prizemoney far in advance of that she'd picked up anywhere else.

From Miami, it was back to Brisbane, Australia, for a Federation Cup semi-final against Belarus in April. Ash, Now the World No.9, was expected to be the backbone in her partnership with Sam Stosur with her 10-1 singles record and a 16-2 record in doubles in the event.

Ash and Sam sent Australia into their first Fed Cup final in 26 years by taking out the deciding doubles tie against Victoria Azarenka and world No.10 Aryna Sabalenka.

They took out a thrilling contest 7-5 3-6 6-2, after Ash had won her two singles matches, including a 7-6 6-3 victory over the two-time Australian Open champion Victoria Azarenka and cruising to a 6-2 6-2 win over Sabalenka.

Sam had lost a draining near three-hour tussle to Sabalenka and fell to Azarenka 6-2 6-2.

The doubles became the decider.

Ash and Sam took the opening set after breaking at 6-5 up before the Belarusian pair hit back to take the second set 6-3.

But in the final set the Australians turned it on, especially Stosur who seemed to find another gear as her volleying and serve began to dominate, backed up by her trademark forehand winners.

That put the Australian into the final against France in Perth towards the end of the year. Ash left no one in doubt about how she felt playing for Australia.

In her words: “I’ve said right from the start, it’s an honour and privilege to be able to play for Australia. When Mol (team captain Alicia Molik) asked me to play three times during the week, I put my hand up absolutely, do whatever she asks.

“For all of us, I’m so proud of every single person sitting around this table. I think in particular Mol having the belief and the faith in us, knowing that whoever she puts out on the court, we can back in 100 per cent.”

The Federation Cup now on the backburner until later in the year, Ash’s next assignment was Europe for key tournaments in Italy, Spain, France and England, from May through to July, culminating in The Championships on the hallowed grass of Wimbledon.

She made a bright start in Spain, with a straight-sets win over compatriot Daria Gavrilova and advancing to the quarter-finals before going down in straight sets to Simona Halep of Rumania.

After Spain, Ash went to Italy the next week and suffered a disappointing quarter-final 2-6 3-6 loss to Kristina Mladenovic of France. However, her second-round tough three-set win over Viktoria Kuzmova of Slovakia and results of other players pushed her up to No.8 in the rankings and seedings for the French Open.

The loss to Mladenovic was to be her last in 12 matches before taking on Wimbledon and claiming two significant titles on the way.

The clay courts of Roland Garros in France beckoned in

May. Ash dropped only two sets on her way to the final. Five of her six wins were against Americans, including Madison Keys.

In a surprisingly one-sided contest, Ash ended Australia's 46-year wait for a French Open singles title by thrashing Czech teenager Marketa Vondrousova.

Ash got off to a strong start and never looked back, winning 6-1 6-3 after only 70 minutes to claim her maiden Grand Slam title.

Next stop Birmingham and on to grass for a warm-up for Wimbledon and a shot at becoming World No.1 after her French Open win took her to No.2.

She drew a tough opponent in the first round in China's SaiSai Zheng but progressed relatively comfortably through early rounds to encounter American Venus Williams, in the twilight of her career but still considered a dangerous opponent. Ash got through that match unscathed to face Czech Barbora Strycova in the semi-final. A two-set win put her into the final against friend and doubles partner Julia Goerges. Another two-set victory was the outcome and Ash had taken the Birmingham title without dropping a set in five matches.

With world No.1 Naomi Osaka (Japan) bowing out in the quarter-finals to Yulia Putintseva in straight sets, Ash Barty became the No.1 woman tennis player in the world as at 1 July.

She stayed at the top until the North American swing and a first-round exit in Toronto, Canada, where she was top seed, that saw her eventually losing the No.1 ranking to Naomi Osaka.

The chance to regain the top spot came in the US open

a fortnight later at Flushing Meadows when the points system worked in her favour after Osaka went out in the fourth round, as did Ash.

Osaka had more at stake in the points, having gone in as defending champion and carrying a swag of points she needed to hold on to from the previous year's success.

As Ash headed to the year-end Asian swing her win-loss record for the year was 39-6 in singles and 18-4 in doubles.

Her itinerary in Asia included the season-ending WTA finals in Shenzhen, the first Australian woman to qualify for the field of eight since Sam Stosur in 2012 when the finals were in Istanbul.

The hope that she would see out the year as World No.1 remained alive as she began the year-end Asian circuit at Wuhan.

A bye in the first round of the Wuhan Open in the last week of September pitted Ash against 2017 Wuhan winner Caroline Garcia, of France, in the second round. Ash appeared rusty in the first set after a lay-off at the end of the US Open and lost it 4-6. But she quickly found her range and took the match 4-6 6-4 6-1.

Ash's rival for top spot going to Wuhan, Karolina Pliskova (Czech Republic), also won her second-round match but bowed out in the next round when she needed to stay "alive" in the tournament longer than Ash to overtake her at the top.

Ash went into the semi-finals after a high-quality three-set win over Petra Martic (Croatia), 7-6 (8-6 tiebreak) 3-6

6-3, but fell to Aryna Sabalenka, 5-7 4-6. Ash was treated for a calf injury during the match but didn't use it as an excuse.

In her words: "I'm sure (the injury) is nothing that is too alarming. I tried to do the best that I could to protect it in a way without letting it affect my tennis too much. Overall, Aryna was the better player. She was able to control her service games a lot better. I felt at times I was hanging on a little bit. I had to take a lot of risks today to try to manage where I was at. I was more in the match than I deserved to be.

Sabalenka went on to win the tournament. The early departure of Pliskova combined with Ash's repeat of the previous year's semi-final appearance meant she didn't lose ranking points and retained the No.1 position of the 1000 players in the world rankings as the tour moved to Beijing.

Pliskova bowed out in the first round of the Beijing Open, losing to Jelena Ostapenko (Latvia) and failing to defend her 120 points from the previous year. That cleared the way for Ash to remain World No.1, no matter how she fared in Beijing; she did not have any points to defend and entered the draw in the second round.

After Beijing she was on her way to the WTA finals in Shenzhen at the end of October and into the first week of November where the winner would pocket $US4.75 million of the record $US14 million prizemoney on offer.

20

# ASH'S 2019 SINGLES RECORD

Three titles (Miami, French and Birmingham), won 37 of 44 matches from January to June on her way to becoming No.1, including 12 in succession after a straight-sets 2-6 3-6 loss in the quarter-finals in Rome on 16 May.

## JANUARY

HOPMAN CUP: After a first round win in the Hopman Cup (Perth, indoor) right at the end of 2018 defeating Alize Cornet of France 7-5 6-3.

Ash began 2019 with another Hopman Cup victory:

Jan 2 — defeated Aliza Cornet (France) 7-5 6-3; defeated Garbine Muguruza (Spain) 7-5 6-3.

Jan 4 — Lost to Angelique Kerber (Germany) 3-6 4-6.

WTA SINGLES SYDNEY (hardcourt):

Jan 8 — defeated Jelena Ostapenko (Latvia) 6-3 6-3.

Jan 9 — defeated Simona Halep (Romania) 6-4 6-4.

Jan 10 — defeated Elise Mertens (Belgium) 6-3 6-3.

Jan 11 — defeated Kiki Bertens (Netherlands) 6-7 6-4 7-5.

Jan 12 — lost to Petra Kvitova (Czech Republic) 1-6 7-5 6-7.

AUSTRALIAN OPEN, Melbourne (hardcourt):

Jan 14 — defeated Luksika Kumkhum (Thailand) 6-2 6-2.

Jan 16 — defeated Yafan Wang (China) 6-2 6-3.

Jan 18 — defeated Maria Sakkari (Greece) 7-5 6-1.

Jan 20 — defeated Maria Sharapova (Russia) 4-6 6-1 6-4.

Jan 22 — lost to Petra Kvitova (Czech Republic) 1-6 4-6.

## FEBRUARY

FEDERATION CUP (World Group, Australia v USA, Asheville, North Carolina, hardcourt):

Feb 10 — defeated Sofia Kenin 6-1 7-6.

Feb 11 — defeated Madison Keys 6-4 6-1.

## MARCH

INDIAN WELLS USA (hardcourt):

Mar 9 — defeated Tatjana Maria (Germany) 6-4 6-4.

Mar 11 — defeated Jennifer Brady (USA) 6-3 6-2.

Mar 13 — lost to Elina Svitolina (Ukraine) 6-7 7-5 4-6.

WTA MIAMI (hardcourt):

Mar 22 — defeated Dayana Yastremska (Ukraine) 6-4, 6-4.

Mar 24 — defeated Sam Stosur (Australia) 6-0 6-3.

Mar 26 — defeated Kiki Bertens (Netherlands) 4-6 6-3 6-2.

Mar 27 — defeated Petra Kvitová (Czech Republic ) 7-6 (8-5) 3-6 6-2.

Mar 29 — defeated Anett Kontaveit (Estonia) 6-3 6-3.

Mar 31 — defeated Karolina Pliskova (Czech Republic) 7-6 (7-1) 6-3.

## APRIL

FEDERATION CUP singles, World Group (Brisbane) v Belarus:

April 20 — defeated Aryna Sabalenka 6-2 6-2.

April 21 — defeated Victoria Azarenka 7-6 6-3.

## MAY

MUTUA MADRID OPEN:

May 4 — defeated Daria Gavrilova (Australia) 6-1 6-2.

May 7 — defeated Danielle Collins (USA) 6-1 1-6 6-1.

May 8 — defeated Yulia Putintseva (Kazakhstan) 4-6 6-1 6-2.

May 9 — quarter-final, lost to Simona Halep 5-7 5-7.

ROME, Internazionali BNL d'Italia:

May 14 — defeated Viktoria Kuzmova (Slovakia) 4-6 6-3 6-4.

May 16 — Lost to Kristina Mladenovic (France) 2-6 3-6.

## MAY-JUNE

FRENCH OPEN, Roland Garros:

May 27 — defeated Jessica Pegula (USA) 6-3 6-3.

May 30 — defeated Danielle Collins (USA) 7-5 6-1.

June 2 — defeated Andrea Petkovic (Germany) 6-3 6-1.

June 3 — defeated Sofia Kenin (USA) 6-3 3-6 6-0.

June 6 — quarter-finals, defeated Madison Keys (USA) 6-3 7-5.

June 7 — semi-finals, defeated Amanda Anisimova (USA) 6-7 6-3 6-3.

June 9 — final, defeated Markéta Vondroušová (Czech Republic) 6-1 6-3.

## JUNE

BIRMINGHAM, Nature Valley Classic:

June 19 — defeated Donna Vekic (Croatia) 6-3 6-4.

June 20 — defeated Jennifer Brady (USA) 6-3 6-1.

June 22 — quarter-finals, defeated Venus Williams (USA) 6-4 6-3.

June 22 — semi-finals, defeated Barbora Strŷcová (Czech) 6-4 6-4.

June 23 — final, defeated Julia Görges (Germany) 6-3 7-5.

Monday June 24: The new world rankings have Ashleigh at No.1 as she heads into July after her win at the Nature Valley Classic in Birmingham, her sixth WTA title. Previous No.1 Naomi Osaka is relegated to No.2. Ash started the season ranked 15.

## JULY

WIMBLEDON:

July 2 — defeated Saisai Zheng (China) 6-4 6-2.

July 4 — defeated Alison Van Uytvanck (Belgium) 6-1 6-3.

July 6 — defeated Harriet Dart (Great Britain) 6-1 6-1.

July 8 — lost to Alison Riske (USA) 6-3 2-6 3-6.

After Wimbledon, Ash's win/loss record is 41/7 and a career record of 236/89 – 46/24 on clay, 119/43 on hardcourts, 12/2 indoors and 49/16 on grass.

## AUGUST

TORONTO:

Bye in the first round.

Aug 2 — lost to American Sofia Kenin 7-6 3-6 4-6.

CINCINATTI:

Bye in the first round.

Aug 15 — defeated Maria Sharapova (Russia) 6-4 6-1.

Aug 16 — defeated Anett Kontaveit (Estonia) 4-6 7-5 7-5.

Aug 17 — defeated Maria Sakkari (Greece) 5-7 6-2 6-0.

Aug 18 — lost to wildcard entry Svetlana Kuznetsova (Russia) in straight sets 2-6 4-6.

EXHIBITION MATCH, US:

Aug 22 — Ash played rising American teenage star Coco Gauff in an exhibition match at the Winston-Salem Open. Ash lost to the 15-year-old 4-6 6-2 and 8-10 (modified tie breaker set).

## AUGUST-SEPTEMBER

US OPEN:

Aug 27 — defeated Zarina Diyas (Kazakhstan) 1-6 6-3 6-2.

Aug 29 — defeated Lauren Davis (USA) 6-2 7-6 (7/2).

Aug 31 — defeated Maria Sakkari of Greece 7-5 6-3.

Sept 2 — lost to Wang Qiang (China) 2-6 4-6.

Wang's defence and counterattack proved difficult for Barty to deal with. Questions were asked about whether Ash's two-and-a-half hour doubles match the previous day had taken a toll. The loss put Ash's return to No.1 in jeopardy, however the early exits by defending US Open champion and newly reinstated World No.1 Naomi Osaka and World No.3 challenger Karolina Pliskova, meant Ash's fourth-round appearance, even though a loss, returned her to world No.1 immediately after the US Open.

That also meant she was the first to qualify for the Porsche Race to Shenzhen WTA singles finals in October-November, where the top eight singles and doubles pairs from the year were to compete for a record $US14 million prizemoney.

## SEPTEMBER

WUHAN OPEN:

Sept 23 — defeated Caroline Garcia (France) 4-6, 6-4, 6-1.
Sept 24 — defeated Sofia Kenin (US) 6-3, 7-5.
Sept 25 — defeated Petra Martic (Croatia) 7-6, 3-6, 6-3.
Sept 26 — (final) lost to Aryna Sabalenka (Belarus) 6-7, 4-6.
A bye in the first round put Ash into the second round for her first match against Caroline Garcia of France. After dropping the first set, Ash recovered to win 4-6 6-4 6-1. That put her into the quarter-final against Petra Martic, Ash taking that match 7-6 3-6 6-3 to earn a place in the semi-finals against defending Wuhan champion Aryna Sabalenka (Belarus). Sabelenka proved too good on the day, defeating Ash 7-5 6-4, almost a repeat of the 2018 result when Sabelenka won 7-6 6-4. Sabalenka went on to successfully defend her Wuhan title. Ash, however, retained the world number one spot.

## OCTOBER

BEIJING OPEN:

Oct 1 — defeated Yulia Putinseva (Kazakhstan) 6-4, 6-2.
Oct 2 — defeated Saisai Zheng (China) 6-3, 6-7, 6-2.
Oct 4 — defeated Petra Kvitova (Czech Republic) 4-6, 6-4, 6-3.
Oct 5 — defeated Kiki Bertens (Netherlands) 6-3, 3-6, 7-6.

Oct 6 — (final) lost to Naomi Osaka (Japan) 6-3, 3-6, 2-6. Ash's fighting qualities were not displayed more forcibly than her march to the final of the Beijing Open. She faced defeat in several games and was even down to match point in her semi-final against Kiki Bertens of The Netherlands. But she kept fighting back with some matches that extended beyond two hours.

A bye in the first round pitted her against Yulia Putintseva (Kazakhstan) and Ash prevailed comfortably 6-4 6-3, to meet local favourite Zheng Saisai. Ash took the first set in quick-time, 6-3, but lost the second 6-7 in a tiebreak. It was time for a fightback and she rallied to win the decider 6-2 and seal a spot in the quarter-finals of a WTA event for the ninth time.

Overcoming Petra Kvitova was always going to be a challenge with the Czech player ahead 4-1 in their past five clashes.

Former Wimbledon champion Kvitova broke Ash once in the first set to take it 6-4. But Ash as she has done many times drew on her fighting qualities to hit back in the second set, taking it 6-4 and beating off five break points. She took the third set 6-3 for her 51st win for the year.

That set up a semi-final clash against No.8 Kiki Bertens who had not beaten Ash in four meetings. Ash was down a match point at one stage but held on for a gripping 3-6 6-3 7-6 victory.

The final against Naomi Osaka of Japan was also an epic battle of contracting styles — guile against power. Ash took the first set 6-3 with just one break. Osaka got the only break in the second set to take it 6-3 and broke again early in the decider. It was going to take Ash's best fightback to save the match when Osaka went 3-1 and then 5-2 after another break as Ash's unforced error count mounted. A comeback wasn't to be, but though losing Ash was still No.1 and on her way to Shenzhen to contest the WTA finals at year-end, just more than 1,000 ranking points clear of No.2, Karolina Pliskova, and almost 1,500 points clear of Osaka who moved up to No.3. The October WTA rankings saw 11 Australian women in the top 200, with Ash the standard-bearer.

## OCTOBER – NOVEMBER

SHENZHEN WTA FINALS (round robin then finals):
Oct 27 — defeated Belinda Bencic (Switzerland) 5-7, 6-1, 6-2.
Oct 29 — lost to Kiki Bertens (Netherlands) 6-3, 3-6, 4-6.
Oct 31 — defeated Petra Kvitova (Czech Republic) 6-4, 6-2.
Nov 2 — defeated Karolina Pliskova (Czech Republic) 4-6, 6-2, 6-3.
Nov 3 — defeated Elina Svitolina (Ukraine) 6-4, 6-3.

FEDERATION CUP v FRANCE:
Nov 9 – defeated Caroline Garcia 6-0, 6-0.
Nov 10 – lost to Kristina Mladenovic 6-2, 4-6, 6-7.

27

# JUNIOR CAREER

The highlight of Ash's junior career was winning the girls' singles at Wimbledon in 2011.

She started playing on the ITF Junior circuit in 2009, aged thirteen. In her first singles event she reached the second round at Waikato Bays ITF and The New Zealand 18 and Unders Indoor Championship.

She won her first title at the Grade 4 Australian International before she was fourteen.

She reached a career-high ITF world junior ranking of No.2, playing singles and doubles.

She continued playing on the lower tier circuit until the end of 2010, with a record of 24 wins and two losses in her five events that year. She also picked up a Grade 2 title in Thailand.

She played her first junior Grand Slam event in 2011 at the Australian Open, where she lost her opening match to third seed Lauren Davis.

After that, she won singles and doubles at two Grade 1 events, the Sarawak Chief Minister's Cup in Malaysia in March and the Belgian International Junior Championships in May.

She bowed out of the 2011 French Open in 2011 in the second round. Then, at age fifteen, she went on to the Junior Wimbledon tournament where she became the second Australian winner of the Girls Singles, after Debbi Freeman in 1980, and the first Australian girl to win any junior Grand Slam singles title since Jelena Dokic at the 1998 US Open.

She lost only one set, to American Madison Keys in the third round. She defeated third seed Irina Khromacheva in the final. Ash started slowly in her match against the 16-year-old Russian, trailing 1-4 in the first set before fighting back to win the match 7-5 7-6. South Australian Luke Saville made it a junior Wimbledon double for Australia by winning the boys' singles.

Ash went on to the US Open, the last Grand Slam of the year and reached the semi-finals where she lost to top seed Caroline Garcia.

She also won two more Grade 1 titles in doubles that season, one at Roehampton in the lead-up to Wimbledon and the other at the Canadian Open in the lead-up to the US Open.

To finish the season, she teamed with Belinda Woolcock to win the Junior Federations Cup for Australia.

In 2012, she won ITF titles in Sydney, Mildura, Nottingham and Traralgon.

She finished her junior career in 2012, with runner up results in both singles and doubles at the Torneo International in Italy.

28

# DOUBLES CAREER

Ashleigh Barty made her singles and doubles main draw debuts on the WTA Tour in early 2012 at the Brisbane International.

The 15-year-old Ash was given a wild card into the Brisbane event and after discussions with former tour players Nicole Pratt and Jason Stoltenberg opted for doubles. It was recommended she approach Casey Dellacqua who at that time was ranked in the top 40 in singles and had won a major doubles title.

She sent a message to Casey and said afterwards: "I thought it probably would be a good match-up with the personality, more so than the tennis, to start off with."

Casey accepted and they faced up to top seeds Natalie Grandin and Vladimira Uhlirova in the first round, knocking them out in a tie-break. They went on to the semi-finals before being eliminated.

Ash said: "Just from the start we gelled really well. And then our second tournament we won a 75 ($US75,000 ITF tournament) in Japan. And the next year was 2013 so that was our big year."

She had a variety of partners for tournaments in Launceston, Ipswich and Hobart without great success until she linked up again with Casey Dellacqua. They advanced to the final of the Australian Open where they lost 2-6 6-3 2-6 to Italian pair Sara Errani and Roberta Vinci.

Ash and Casey lost their doubles match to the Czech pair in the Fed Cup that year.

Ash joined another Australian, Anastasia Rodionova and they reached the semi-finals in Charleston (USA), going down to Kristina Mladenovic (France) and Lucy Safarina (Czech) 1-6 4-6 after accounting for the second seeds in the quarter-finals.

Ash and Casey reunited for the French Open but were eliminated in the first round.

Success came later in 2013 at Birmingham when Ash and Casey went all the way to snare their first title, defeating Cara Black (Zimbabwe) and Marina Erakovic (New Zealand) 7-5 6-4.

They played eight tournaments together. At Wimbledon and the US Open, Ash and Casey defeated three of the top 10 seeds at both, including the No.2 seeds.

Their effort in Wimbledon that year was most impressive. They had five fairly convincing wins before defeating Su-Wei Hsieh (Taiwan) and Shuai Peng (China) 7-6 7-1 to take their first Grand Slam event.

Ash and Casey went on to the US Open and also reached the final, this time going down in a tight three-setter to Czech pair Andrea Sestina Hlaveckova and Lucie Hradeck 7-6 1-6 4-6.

By the end of 2013, Ash's WTA doubles ranking had risen from No.129 to No.12.

In 2014, Ash and Casey had little success until March when they paired to win the doubles match of the Federation Cup tie over German pair Julia Goerges and Anna-Lena Groenefeld in three sets.

May in Strasbourg saw Ash and Casey collect another title, but they were ousted from the French Open by Italians Errani and Vinci in three sets in the quarter-finals and ousted at Birmingham in the semi-finals in straight sets by Americans Raquel Atawo and Abigail Spears.

Wimbledon again saw them fall victim to the Italians but this time they managed to claim a set in the three-set final.

They finished the year bowing out in the first round of the US Open. Ash didn't reappear in doubles matches again until 2016, just for one tour match, paring with Brit Laura Robson for a first-round exit on the Wimbledon grass.

Then came Ash's break from tennis and it was not until 2017 that Ash and Casey got together again for the French Open where they reached the final, becoming the first Australian team to reach the finals of all four Grand Slam doubles events.

Success came in March in Malaysia at the Kuala Lumpur tournament. They took the title with a straight sets win over Nicole Melichar (USA) and Makoto Ninomiya (Japan).

Two months later they were trophy winners again at

Strasbourg, defeating Taiwanese pair Hao-Ching Chan and Latisha Chan in straight sets.

In June Ash and Casey made it all the way to the final of the French Open, going down to top-seeds Bethanie Mattek-Sands (USA) and Lucie Safarova (Czech) 2-6 1-6.

Birmingham saw Ash and Casey take another title in a three-setter, 10-8 in the third over Chinese pair Hao-Ching Chan and Shuai Zhang. That was to be their last success for 2017.

They made a bold showing at Eastbourne, before going down in straight sets to Latisha Chan and Martina Hingis who was making a reappearance at 38 years of age.

Wimbledon saw a tight match, going down in three sets to Russian No.2 seeds Ekaterina Makarova and Elena Vesnina 6-4 4-6 and 11-13 in a marathon decider.

At the end of the year Ash was ranked No.11 in doubles. She began 2018 in Brisbane with Casey, losing in the third round, and going out in the second round in Melbourne.

Success came in the Federation Cup tie with Rumania in February, Ash and Casey winning the doubles 6-3 6-4.

There was no more doubles title joy for Ash until she joined Coco Vandeweghe at the Miami tournament in April, taking the final 6-2 6-2 over Czech pair Barbora Krejcikova and Katerina Siniakova.

Ash followed up in Rome when she and Demi Schuurs (Netherlands) defeated the Czechs Sestini and Hlavachova in straight sets.

They were successful again in Montreal over Chan and Makarova, winning in three sets, 10-8 in the decider.

Coco Vandeweghe re-joined Ash for the US Open doubles in September and they went all the way, needing to win two tie-break sets in a three-set nail-biter over Timea Babos (Hungary) and Kristina Mladenovic (France) 3-6 7-6 7-6.

Ash played in the elite doubles WTA play-offs in November in Singapore with Coco Vandeweghe who withdrew from Zhuhai because of injury. They won their first round match but lost narrowly in the semi-finals to Timea Babos (Hungary) and Kristina Mladenovic (France) 7-6 3-6 8-10.

Ash finished 2018 ranked No.7 in doubles.

In 2019, Ash played several doubles matches with Victoria Azarenka (Belarus).

In Madrid in May, they were unseeded and lost in the round of 16 to the number eight seeds Anna-Lena Groenefeld and Demi Schuurs.

They got their revenge in Rome a week later, reversing the Madrid loss over Goenefeld and Schuurs, winning 4-6 6-0 (10-3 in the modified format for the decider).

It was a successful defence of the 2018 title for Ash, who partnered Schuurs that year.

Rome was an impressive performance by the pairing; they defeated the tournament's number one seeds, Czech duo Barbora Krejcikova and Katerina Siniakova in the semi-final, and fifth seeded duo Hsie Su-wei and Barbora Strycova in the second round.

Ash and Azarenka reached the third round of the French open before going down in three sets to Sam Stosur and Shuai Zheng.

Ash joined Julia Goerges in Birmingham but conceded in the third round by walkover after winning their two earlier matches in straight sets. The pair opted to get ready for their singles decider instead of playing doubles.

Azarenka returned to partner Ash in doubles at Wimbledon, but they defaulted after winning their first two round matches, Ash citing a need to rest her arm after some testing tournaments in the lead-up.

By the end of Wimbledon in July, and after playing 12 events, Ash was ranked No.6 in WTA doubles.

She and Azaranka teamed up for the US Open, ranked No.9 and seeded eight.

They defeated Monica Niculescu (Romania) and Margarita Gasparyan (Russia) 4-6 6-1 6-1 in the first round, then defeated Nadiia Kichenok (Ukraine) and Abigail Spears (United States) 6-3 3-6 7-6 (tiebreak) in the second round, in a two-and-a-half-hour battle to go into the third round.

There they disposed of the precocious young American teenagers Coco Gauff and Caty McNally 6-0 6-1 in just 47 minutes to earn a place in the quarter-finals against the top seeds, Timea Babos (Hungary) and Kristina Mladenovic (France).

Ash and Azarenka dropped the first set but hit back to win their way to the semi-final 2-6 7-5 6-1.

They made short work of unseeded pair Victoria Kuzmova (Slovakia) and Alison Van Uytvanck (Belgium) in their semi-final, winning 6-0 6-1.

That took them to the final against No.3 seeded pair, Elise Mertens (Belgium) and Aryna Sabelenka (Belarus).

Ash had the chance of becoming the first woman in 12 years to win back-to-back US Open doubles titles, having won in 2018 with American Coco Vandeweghe.

It was not to be; Ash and Azarenka were unable to convert their dominance for most of the match into claiming a set from the number three seeds, going down 5-7 5-7.

However, the result saw them rise to No.9 in the year-long rankings, just one place out of automatically qualifying for the WTA end-of-year doubles play-offs in Shenzhen.

In 2021 Ash teamed up with American Jennifer Brady. After bowing out early in Melbourne they went on to win their first WTA title as a team with a 6-4 5-7, 10-5 win over top-seeded Americans Bethanie Mattek-Sands and Desirae Krawczyk.

Ash and Storm Sanders joined for the summer Olympic Games in Tokyo (held in 2021 after being postponed). The Australians lost in the quarter-finals.

29

# MIXED DOUBLES

Ash has made limited appearances in mixed doubles, with no tournament titles.

Her first venture into a Grand Slam mixed was in 2012 with Benjamin Mitchell. The Australians were put out in the first round by Bernard Tomic (Australia) and Jelena Jankovic (Serbia).

She partnered Tomic in the Hopman Cup in Perth in 2012-13 for just one win.

There were three wins at Wimbledon in 2012 with fellow Australian John Peers before they fell to Bruna Soares (Brazil) and Lisa Raymond (Australia) in the quarter-finals, losing two tie-break sets.

Joining John Peers again in 2013, the Australians contested several tournaments without luck through to 2018, not playing in 2014-15. Their best result was reaching the third round in the US Open in 2014.

Ash joined Matthew Ebden in Australia's Hopman Cup team in 2018-19 and they won two of their three matches, including a straight sets victory over German pair Angelique Kerber and Alexander Zverev in a modified format.

Ash and John Peers represented Australia in the Tokyo Olympics mixed doubles, claiming the bronze medal.

# 30

# CRICKET

Ash Barty played cricket at three levels in 2015-16, for Western Suburbs in the Brisbane women's competition, Queensland Fire in the national women's one-day series and Brisbane Heat in the women's Big Bash.

### Western Suburbs

Matches: 26; Batting Average 30.28; Highest: 107.

Bowling: 8 wickets. Average: 18.75. Best: 2/12.

Ash was a hit for her club side, scoring an explosive 63 not out from 60 balls against University of Queensland in her first T20 game, and taking 2 for 13 from four overs of medium-paced bowling.

She last played on 20 February 2016.

### Queensland Fire

Ash began training with the Queensland Fire squad in July 2015. In November, she was selected in the Fire one-day team for a match in a Women's National Cricket League one-day match in Adelaide, where she made only one run and didn't bowl.

## Brisbane Heat

The Heat signed Ash after two games for her club side. In her first game for the Heat on 5 December 2015, she scored 39 from 27 balls, the second highest in the opening round of the season, when the Heat played the Melbourne Stars. The match report noted: "She didn't face a ball until the 13th over, saw Lauren Winfield and Sammy-Jo Johnson fall soon afterwards, and had to keep calm while accumulating 9 from 15 balls. Then she started working twos, before branching out into boundaries and finishing with a six down the ground."

Her other scores for the season were, 1, 7 not out, 0, 1, 17 and 3. Her last game was on 16 January 2016.

Brisbane Heat coach Andy Richards described Ash as very humble. She doubted her cricketing abilities.

She started slowly but Richards said she could have developed into a top Australian player.

"I think her first two bats at club level she was out first ball and then second ball," Richards said.

"I think about her fifth or sixth innings in she scored a hundred in a T20 game. She's the most extraordinary individual. She has talent to burn."

Richards, speaking about her early training sessions: "I chucked her on a bowling machine. She hit about 150-odd balls and didn't nick any of them. Middled most of them. It was quite startling, even if she wasn't technically correct," he said.

"Hitting thousands of tennis balls is a perfect base for

cricket." He lamented her return to tennis: "We miss her. We would love to have her in our game. I have no doubt whatsoever (she could have played for Australia)."

Queensland Fire teammate and Australian player Delissa Delissa Kimmince: "Ash didn't look like a tennis-player-trying-to-be-a-cricket-player in the nets. She had great hand-eye co-ordination, obviously, but her technique was also pretty sound, particularly hitting down the ground and through midwicket and mid-on. She picked the ball up quickly and had a nice, clean bat swing. But the thing that really stood out was her work ethic."

31

# WIT AND WISDOM OF ASH BARTY

## HER INSPIRATION

Throughout her triumphant campaign at Wimbledon in 2021, Ash wore a FILA dress inspired by Evonne Goolagong Cawley's 1971 Wimbledon outfit that was designed by the legendary Ted Tingling. It was a tribute to the person she so admires as an achiever, friend and mentor.

"I hope I made Evonne proud," Ash said during an emotional victory speech.

She told an International Women's Day event in 2019: "Evonne Goolagong Cawley has inspired me on and off the court since I was a young girl. Evonne's outstanding achievements and her passion for helping the Indigenous community are two things I admire."

The Barty family has provided inspiration, too.

"I think I've just tried to live by my values that my parents instilled in me. I mean, it's more important to be a good person than it is a good tennis player," Ash said after winning Wimbledon.

"Being able to learn from my parents and my siblings, my

family, was a massive part of my upbringing.

"I think being a good human being is absolutely my priority every single day."

Ash also drew some inspiration from another Indigenous athlete, Cathy Freeman, when she returned to tennis after an 11-month COVID-19 pandemic lay-off, amid some chatter about holding on to the No. 1 ranking through that non-playing period.

"I think her (Cathy's) analogy, particularly through the Sydney Olympics, was one of the best I have ever heard," Ash said. "Her picturing herself as a young girl inside a house and seeing the storm outside, you can see it but you don't hear it. That is really effective and incredible.

"For me it is about accepting that there is noise and extra attention and talk but ultimately that doesn't change how I hit a tennis ball, that doesn't change how I prepare.

"As long as I do all of my processes the right way and make decisions for the right reasons then regardless of whether it is a win or a loss, I sleep well at night knowing we have done everything possible to try and give ourselves the best chance."

## TAKING IT ON THE CHIN

**After being bundled out in the first round of the Tokyo Olympics:** "I can't hide behind that fact that I wanted to do really well here. Today wasn't my day. I get to look forward to playing doubles with Storm and getting in and enjoying the Olympic experience.

**After having to withdraw from the 2021 French Open with an injury:** "It's disappointing to end like this. I've had my fair share of tears this week. It's all good. Everything happens for a reason. There will be a silver lining in this eventually. Once I find out what that is, it'll make me feel a little bit better, but it will be there I'm sure."

**After losing at Wimbledon in 2019:** "It's incredibly tough right now. But in saying that, it's also only a tennis match. I try to do everything I can to win the tennis match. If I don't the sun is still going to come up tomorrow. Today wasn't my day, but that's not going to define us as a team, it's not going to define me as a person. I think that's the most important thing. You always learn a lot more when you lose."

**After losing at the US Open in 2019:** "I don't think a second week of a Slam's a missed opportunity. I think that's a hell of an effort for all Slams, to get to the second week. Yes, I would have loved to have done better, but it wasn't to be. Certainly not something I'm stressed about. I think it's easy to put into perspective because of the person I am and the team I have around me. It doesn't matter whether I win a tennis match or not or I've won a Grand Slam, or I haven't. It's not something that keeps me up at night. I know that I did everything possible to try to prepare as well as I could today and play as well as I could, but in the big moments, it wasn't there.

## IN THE MONEY

After winning world record prizemoney at Shenzhen in 2019: "It's been an incredible season, money aside as it kind of means nothing to me. I know I have the love and the support of my family. I try and work hard every single day to chase my dreams. Regardless of how many zeros is sitting in my bank account, it doesn't change the way I live my life, who I am and how I live as a person. I think even though it's incredible, we're breaking records this week in particular, putting tennis on the map, putting WTA tennis on the map. I feel like we've earned that right to be recognised more as a global sport. For me, it doesn't change a thing. I'm pretty boring. I don't really spend a lot on myself. I obviously like to spoil my family. I'm in a position where I can spoil my niece and nephew. But I'm certainly not one that lives an extravagant lifestyle. I'm pretty happy in my little house at home. I've got everything that I need."

## ADVICE FOR YOUNGSTERS

"Enjoy it, have fun and chase your dreams. All you can do is go out there, work your hardest and chase your dreams."

## THE OLYMPICS

Ash was looking forward to representing Australia in the Olympics in Tokyo in 2020: "Representing your country really is the bee's knees. It's the best thing you can do and to one day, maybe call yourself an Olympian, unbelievable."

## HER TEAM

Ash almost always refers to her team as "us" and "we".

**After winning Wimbledon:** "It was the most incredible feeling I think I've ever experienced on a tennis court," she said. "There was certainly disbelief. I've worked so hard my whole career with my team and with people that mean the most to me to try and achieve my goals and my dreams. To be able to do that today was incredible.

"The fact that we were physically able to get through the past fortnight has been exceptional. I have the most incredible team of people around me and I put full trust in them and knowing that they do absolutely everything possible to give myself trust in my body. I think being able to prove that this fortnight has been incredible, but I certainly have no fears about my fitness.

"Of course, some things will happen; that's normal, that's natural, that's life of being an athlete. But I know that I've got the very best team around me to prepare me in a way as best as we can."

**July 2019 after becoming World No. 1:** "I am extremely lucky to have a team around me, who loves me for Ash Barty the person, not the tennis player. I am extremely lucky to have an amazing family, a truly amazing family that no matter, win lose or draw, the text messages and the face-timing is the same. It is just a really good group of people around me that make the tennis very easy,"

## GETTING AWAY FROM IT ALL

"I had four days break in my off-season. I went fishing, so that was my highlight. All the way from training, it was nice to get up to North Queensland and catch a few nice cold trout and sweetlips, so that was good."

## BEING PART OF THE INDIGENOUS COMMUNITY

"My heritage is really important to me. I've always had that olive complexion and the squished nose, and I just think it's important to do the best I can to be a good role model," she said in one post-match interview.

"The opportunities now that are out there for Indigenous youth all around the nation in Australia is incredible. It's definitely been a steppingstone and a difference for us, not just in the Northern Territory, not just up in North Queensland, but all across the country, there are more opportunities for Indigenous youth to play tennis.

"And not just tennis, to get involved at sport at all levels, all different sport, and that is a pretty beautiful thing. It is not just Indigenous kids. But there is an extra focus for us with Indigenous kids of letting them be able to see that there is a career path in sport. And they'll have the support. They will have the structure.

"And it's pretty amazing, if I can help in any small part, any small way, shape or form, it's pretty incredible."

## HER YEAR OFF (2012)

"I think for me it was a bit of a no-brainer. I needed to take the break. Otherwise I don't think that I'd still be playing the game, to be honest. I think it gave me an opportunity to go and relax and see kind of what it was like to kind of have a normal life, because the tennis tour and the tennis life is very unique. It's very different. It's not for everybody."

And: "I needed some time to refresh mentally more than anything. It became a bit of a slog for me and I wasn't enjoying my tennis as much as I would have liked to. Since returning from the US Open, my team and I have decided that right now it is best for me to take a break from professional tennis. Obviously this has been a very difficult decision with the Australian summer coming up but, after a lot of thought, we feel this is the right decision. I've enjoyed some incredible experiences on the tennis tour and would like to thank my coach, Jason [Stoltenberg], and the team at TA (Tennis Australia) for all of its hard work and support throughout my journey so far."

## COMING BACK TO TENNIS

"Obviously I was very young, but I turn 20 this year (2016) and it's a different perspective on life and tennis in general. I'll be able to do it my way a bit more. If it works, great. If it doesn't, I can't really complain. I've had a phenomenal career for the short time that I did play. I'm just ready to work up that slow grind up the ITFs and hopefully be up with the WTA soon."

**Coach Craig Tyzzer:** "When she approached me and said, 'I'm thinking of giving this another go', the look that she gave me I knew she was deadly serious about coming back."

## THE SHOT SHE'D LIKE TO HAVE

"Roger Federer's second serve. I think it's really underrated."

## ON THE BEERS

**After losing the final in Madrid in 2021:** "We left the courts, we went down to the lobby and had a burger and a beer."

**After winning the French Open:** "We'll kick back with a beer tonight and celebrate."

**And after bowing out of Wimbledon in 2019:** "There might be a beer or two."

## HAVING FUN WITH THE PRESS

The Disney references she slipped into her media conferences:

1. "We kind of came into it thinking like Hakuna Matata." *Lion King.*
2. "I chat to my niece and over and over she just tells me, 'you can go to infinity and beyond'." *Toy Story.*
3. "I think for me sometimes I look at a shot, I play a shot, I think the seaweed is always greener in someone else's lake. I try and think of how else I can win the point. *The Little Mermaid.*

"Well it's caused a little bit of interest hasn't it? It was a way for us to enjoy it and try bring a little bit more energy to the press," she said. I love Disney, I watch it all the time and it's just been a bit of fun for all of us and you guys caught on the third time around."

**Some Hakuna Matata:** "There's no need to look too far into the future or the past. Enjoy the moment." An attitude Summed up by lyrics from "The Lion King": *Hakuna Matata! What a wonderful phrase, Hakuna Matata! Ain't no passing craze. It means no worries, For the rest of your days. It's our problem-free philosophy.*

## AN INSPIRATION TO OTHERS

**Ajla Tomljanovic, Fed Cup teammate and rising star:** "Ash has been just so inspiring, ever since her comeback. What she's done for tennis in Australia is pretty unbelievable. So I think we all just try to draw from her."

And as almost half of Australian entered lockdown amid the COVID-19 pandemic in 2021, Ash became an inspiration for grit and determination to see off the hard times. Australian Sky News host Chris Smith said her Wimbledon victory was "an inspiration to cope".

Smith said on his program: "At a time of stress, separation and anxiety, the nation needed this incredible girl and her inspiring victory. Whoever you are, wherever you are and whatever your situation, we will get through this outbreak."

And speaking of Ash ...

**Her coach, Craig Tyzzer:** "A lot of people talk about her talent and her tennis but talent only gets you so far and it's really her character that has taken her to where she is right now. I'm lucky enough on a daily basis to see what sort of person she is and she's a much better person than she is a tennis player. So, for me, that's been the key."

**Australian tennis icon Rod Laver (winner of 200 singles titles and World No 1 for six years):** "Ash is totally different from all the other players. It was just a thrill to see the way she played. It was just an amazing feeling to think here's this girl, she's not too tall but she has the ability and the guts to keep plugging away. She has a variety of shots, and that's the one thing that makes her totally different from all the other players. Ash has all the game and the competitive juice".

**Sisters Sara and Ali writing on Playersvoice.com when Ash made it to the Top 20:** "On a scale of one to 10, our pride in our sister Ash is a 12. What we're most proud of is the way she carries herself, the person she's become through everything she's experienced and the fact that none of it has changed her. It's a huge amount of pressure to deal with and it's so important when you're a role model for kids, which all these athletes are. But she carries herself with such humility and she's so gracious and generous all the time."

**And:** "At the end of the day, whether she's playing tennis or not, she's the same generous, cheeky, determined little sister we grew up with. We hope she never changes."

**Evonne Goolagong Cawley, the first time she saw Ashley play, in January 2011 when she lost in straight sets to American Lisa Davis:** "That's the first time I've seen her play. "[I knew] just in the first couple of games ... she's really got it. She's got all the strokes. I know she can play better than that, just by watching her. I'll be chatting with her later. I'll tell her she's got it. She's very well rounded in her game. These days, they have the big topspin on the forehand. But she also has slice. She volleys well. It's good to see someone who knows how to volley. I was very impressed with her."

**Jim Joyce, her first coach in Brisbane in a 2010 interview:** "From day one, Ash showed amazing natural ability and concentration. When she was five, her parents rang me and I put her in a group lesson thinking they could bring her back a year later. But she hit a couple of balls back at me and I got her back the next week."

**Alicia Molik, Australian Federation Cup team captain, after Ash's French Open win:** "She has a lot of wow factor in every single match. You don't always see that in tennis players and styles can become monotonous. But that's not part of Ash's game and that's why she's one of the most watchable tennis players. She can do anything and what a way to play tennis when you can pull anything out of your back pocket when it's required. Everyone is acutely aware of what Ash has done. She's doing our country proud and with the way she plays, how exciting she is and the type of person she is, I hope it draws a whole new audience to tennis and a lot of families turn to the game and have a hit."

**Andy Richards, cricket coach:** "I fed her about 150 balls on the bowling machine. She only missed about two or three and the rest of them she hit flush. It was really one of the most extraordinary things from my point of view. She was the most gifted person I have ever seen come across from another sport. We've had a few over time but I've not seen anyone like her before or since. Eventually we had to stop her coming in every day. She got a sore elbow from hitting so many balls because it's a different motion from tennis. She just wanted to get better."

**Rob Barty, Ash's father, on Ash:** "We weren't tennis players. We were golfers. We just thought she was one of these kids that could do everything. We had no idea. People used to say how good she was at tennis but we just thought she was a kid having fun."

**Rob Barty on Ash's return to tennis:** "When she quit I never for one moment thought she would go back to tennis. We never raised it with her during her time off. It wasn't until one day I came home and found about four boxes of new tennis balls at the front door. It was Ash deciding she was going back to play tennis and away she went."

## THE LAST WORD:

**Former world No. 1 Martina Navratilova:** "Barty's slice is more effective on grass than it is on clay. Players on the WTA Tour have a hard time handling slice, because most of them don't want to be inside the baseline. Also with the ball skidding through low, they're hitting a defensive shot from inside the baseline which makes them vulnerable.

"Barty's also a great volleyer — she can even throw in a serve-and-volley play once in a while, and mix it up, maybe chip and charge on a second serve. All of this variety can really get into an opponent's head and create confusion and some cheap mistakes on her opponent's side."

*Quotes are from press reports, interviews after tournaments and WTA, brainyquote.com and ASAP Sports transcripts.*

32

# BRAND BARTY

Ash's success has attracted an array of sponsorship and endorsements that have grown the Ash Barty brand substantially.

She uses racquets manufactured by sports equipment brand Head and her tennis apparel and footwear are sponsored by FILA. She became the part of Rado YoungStar family in 2017 (watches). She joined luxury car brand Jaguar in December 2018. Online video streaming platform Kayo Sports took a sponsorship. Australian food spread brand Vegemite also has her endorsement, as does Banana Boat (sunscreen) and Esmi (skin and hair care).

Ash also has links with Tourism Australia (advertisements and campaigns), Uber Eats (including the Rogue Umpire campaign with Hollywood actor Sacha Baron Cohen and fellow Australian tennis star Nick Kyrgios), YoPRO (ambassador, including the Fuel Your Journey campaign) and Gillette Venus (brand promotion).

In 2020 she backed Indigenous tennis programs in Australia, in association the Australian Tennis Foundation. She has conducted clinics and other sessions with Evonne Goolagong Cawley.

## AWAY FROM THE COURT

Ash's Instagram posts give an insight into some of her life off the tennis courts.

Her profile says: "Aussie Tennis Player, Cricket, Golf, Richmond Tigers (Australian Football League team), Dog Lady, Coffee Lover."

There are lots of tennis photos, including opponents, partners and successes. But she also proudly shows off pictures of her other interests in her life — she's a doting aunt to her sister's daughters and there are pictures of her enjoying the company of family and as a proud godmother.

She loves animals, particularly dogs, four of which feature prominently on her Instagram account. She has served as an ambassador for the RSPCA.

"Dogs are my favourite animal and I have four of them... Rudy, Maxi, Affie and Chino, a mixture of fluff ball breeds," she says. "Coming home and giving them a cuddle on the couch is one of the most simple but enjoyable things for me to do, win or lose they love me exactly the same.

"If anyone is thinking about getting a pet, please check the RSPCA website first, these animals are desperate for good homes."

Her other sporting pastimes include golf, cricket and surfing. She featured in a television segment playing golf with fellow tennis tour player Coco Vandeweghe. She seemed a little hesitant to mention that she had been playing of handicaps of 9 and 10 but was down to 4 when she won her club women's championship. Her club is Brookwater, just out of Brisbane.

She is a big fan of the Richmond Football Club in the Australian Football League and counts Tigers captain Trent Cochin as a good friend.

Her interest in cricket remains, though not as a player. She proudly shows a picture of herself with Australian one-day skipper Aaron Finch on Instagram.

And she keeps in touch with her former teammates from her own playing days and was a keen watcher of Australia's progress on their tour of England that was in progress while the major tennis was under way.

After Australia's first defeat of England, Ash tweeted: "AUSSIES WIN! A stellar performance with the ball is backed up by some gutsy batting and the first two points belong to us!"

She also tweeted support for Australia's Matilda's football team, despite their early exit from the women's soccer World Cup.

She also looks after "her brands" — photos show sponsor names, an RSPCA message and even a Vegemite poster.

Coffee? Undoubtedly, she's a big fan, even having gone to barista school to hone her skills. Favourite brews seem to be a good espresso macchiato or a latte. She posts pictures of some she really likes.

When asked how she felt after a third-round win in the

2019 Australian Open and possible weariness, she replied: "Ice bath, physio, coffee, cricket. I'm good."

After a tennis tournament she's likely to chill out with a beer and a steak, or even go fishing, another pastime she enjoys when the rare chance arises.

During a tournament she maintains a professional approach. Her routine after a match: "As soon as I get off the court, I re-hydrate and warm down on the bike. I then shower and grab something to eat. After eating, I generally see my physio who checks my body and makes sure I have pulled up well. When I get back to the hotel, I try to wind down and relax. To maximise my post-match recovery, I then put a movie on TV and use the Recovery Boots."

Her partner Gary Kissick figures prominently in her life, too, as do friends she has made in tennis, cricket and all her other pursuits. Gary is a trainee PGA professional at Brookwater Golf and Country Club.

"Amazing! The puppies and I are so proud of you baby! Many more to come," Kissick said in an Instagram post after Ash's straight-sets victory over Markéta Vondrousova in the French Open final.

Another sport Ash keeps an eye on is tennis for the disabled. She was among the first on Twitter to congratulate Australian No.1 Dylan Alcott after he won the inaugural quad wheelchair singles final at Wimbledon in 2019. "Onya Dyl!! Never change — you're a bloody legend," she tweeted.

## ON TRAVELLING

As she prepared for the 2019 Australian Open in Melbourne, she gave fans an insight into her travelling life through Escape.com. Travelling is something she has to deal with constantly despite her fear — "I am terrified of heights".

**Essentials:** FILA tennis clothes and shoes (I need different shoes for different surfaces); HEAD racquets, grips, string, and my tennis bag. Lastly, a tube of Vegemite (about $4 worth) to make breakfast anywhere in the world feel more like home. Noise-cancelling headphones.

**Packing:** Hyper-organised. Everything goes in the same spot, in the same pocket, every time. After years of travelling, I have a routine I stick to.

**Packing hack:** "I develop a routine when you pack, so that you put everything in the same spot each time. My routine never changes, so I don't forget anything and can pack very quickly.

"Putting my tennis essentials in first, followed by a few casual outfits. We generally chase the sun in tennis so only play in warm places — though when I am heading to Europe or the UK I always put in a few extra jumpers, just in case. If I do shopping while I'm travelling (very likely) I often need to buy another bag to bring it all home — that, or I try and sneak it into Mum's suitcase if she's travelling with me!"

**A mistake:** Sunscreen exploding in my tennis bag. I now tape all toiletry bottles shut with sports tape.

**Luggage:** A Head (tennis brand) suitcase and Head tennis bag. They're really easy to spot on the carousel and large enough to fit all my clothes and shoes in. I can be away from home for up to eight weeks, so I need large bags and several of them.

**Carry-on tip:** Keep your carry-on bags light and always take a phone charger with you on the plane.

**Travelling outfit:** Casual and comfy — usually tracksuit pants and a hoodie.

**Keeping fit on the road:** Taking compression boots and TheraBands — these let me do my rehab while on the road.

**Go-to travel app:** Tripadvisor or similar to help me find a good coffee spot. Also, Kayo Sports, which allows you to stream live sports, and Spotify, both of which help keep me entertained on the road. (She is an ambassador for Kayo.)

**What I am working on:** Keeping things as light as possible — I'm pretty small, so carrying big bags is extra tough! Also, I need to learn how to pack for a non-tennis trip. Packing a bag with no tennis clothes is a foreign concept for me.

## ON SHAPING UP

**Breakfast:** "Training is a little different to a match, but on a standard day at the moment I usually wake up, have a coffee and either banana or Vegemite on toast, with a yoghurt — that's my standard brekkie. And then straight after practice a piece of fruit to get me through, and a good lunch to set me up for the rest of the day. After training, come four or five o'clock, it's an afternoon coffee and another piece of fruit before I go home and cook up a pretty simple, basic dinner with four or five veg. It's what I grew up with."

**Training (In the lead up to a tournament):** It's 45 minutes of body preparations work in the morning, whether it be stretching or working on a few weaker areas. And then straight into a bit of a movement session before we go out and practice for two hours. Then we have a bit of lunch and rest before either a gym or condition session in the afternoon, followed by a rehab session. And then sometimes as well we sneak a second on-court session if we need to do any extras. So, it's a lot of hours on the court and in the gym.

**Pressure:** I'm very lucky to have a very genuine team around me filled with amazing people. My family keep me very level-headed and grounded. And obviously they've had all the experiences in the world between them so I think they're able to share that with me. And then it's just a lot of practice. Obviously, we've played a lot of tennis matches over our lives, and you try to learn from each other. I try and keep my cards close to my chest on the tennis court and try not to show too much emotion. Ideally, you're trying not to give your opponent any extra edge.

**Mental health:** Her issues with being alone on tour at a young age led her to take a break in which she ended up playing cricket. She took medication for depression for two years. Evonne Goolagong Cawley sent her a text when she heard was taking a break: "Hey, darl, good decision. Go and wet a line." She did but ended up doing something completely different — playing professional cricket. Rest days are important to her now, particularly between tournaments. "I'm my own boss now. If I need a day off, I need a day off." She will go home and recharge. "That makes me feel 10,000 times better."

## IMPORTANCE OF HERITAGE

Indigenous publications have used their own dictionary to translate her tennis skills into their language: Her forehand is a like "malub" — lightning; her smash is like "miribi" — thunder; her backhand slice is like "djuran" — running water; and she glides around the court like "mugan" — a ghost.

Her great-grandmother was a member of the Ngaragu people from southern NSW and north-eastern Victoria and Ash has formally registered with the clan.

"My heritage is really important to me." She has referred in interviews to her appearance. "I've always had that olive complexion and the squished nose and I just think it's important to do the best I can to be a good role model," she once said in an interview.

**Getting her family involved:** Ash's father Rob, though not a tennis player, has embraced his daughter's hope for future tennis stars.

Rob Barty went on the road in 2020 to share the secrets of bringing up a Grand Slam champion who is a humble and likeable role model.

Tennis Queensland said 14 clubs from Edmonton to Dalby had visits from Rob who talked about the ups and downs of guiding his daughter to the top of professional tennis.

"Ash and I really wanted to do this, but Ash is driving it. It is her small way of giving back to the tennis community in her home state. We want to help other parents and players by telling them what it's like to be a professional player, including the pitfalls," Rob said. "I talk about what we did from when Ash was six years old. I don't tell people what to do, just give them something to consider by explaining the system we used, which is basically keep Mum and Dad out of it and leave it to the professionals."

33

# RESPECT IS THE WORD

Words that describe Ash Barty might include humble, self-effacing, honest. Words that describe her tennis include gritty, determined, fiercely competitive.

But there's one overriding sentiment that surrounds her: Respect. Respect of her and her respect of others. For example, her venture around the world in 2021 raised the issue of vaccination to protect against the COVID-19 pandemic.

Ash was keen to take up WTA offers for vaccination in the US. But she was just as keen to make sure she and her team didn't "jump the queue".

"Tyz (her coach) and I were able to get the vaccine in Charleston (US) and the way the system was working in South Carolina, it was important for me to know that we weren't jumping the queue and we were able to get the vaccine, as we were a lot of other players," she said. "They had organised through a certain pharmacy that had extras, and that was important to me knowing that those who were the most vulnerable were able to get it first."

Ash may have fierce rivals for tournament crowns and world rankings but you don't hear her speak any ill of opponents.

There have been times of great disappointment and sometimes an outsider would believe she would be within her rights to challenge someone else's acts on court at critical stages, such as a prolonged medical or toilet break or a disputed call. Or even seeing her matches scheduled to lesser courts.

But Ash takes it all on the chin and moves on.

You don't hear anything ill said of Ash by her conquerors or her vanquished. Yes, there might be some emotional reaction to a loss or even a victory but Ash leaves a favourable impression no matter what.

She once explained: "I understand that I am in the public eye and I have to set the right example, I want to do everything possible to win a tennis match, but (if you lose) at the end of the day, you shake your opponent in the hand, you look them in the eye and say 'too good, mate'."

Ash embraces the game and in fact reaches out to opponents rather than isolate from them.

She raised eyebrows in New York during her preparation for at the 2021 US Open when she invited rising Polish star Iga Swiatek to practice with her. She did the same with Naomi Osaka in the lead up to the French Open.

Swiatek, ranked No. 8 in the world at the time, said she was impressed by Ash's ability to stay calm even when things weren't going her way. "It's really inspiring. Practising with Ash is different because you can see her mentality and the way she treats things.

"When she makes a mistake, she's not frustrated. She doesn't seem to [get frustrated]," Swiatek said in a WTA interview. "Even when she is frustrated, she uses it to play better and better. So I'm trying to learn from her. I think I need a few more years to understand completely how to get there. But she's a great player to watch and take some lessons from her."

One of Ash's main rivals for the No. 1 world ranking, Belarusian Aryna Sabalenka, said of Ash: "What she's doing, it's unbelievable. She's playing really well. Her game is really tough. She's a really tough opponent for most of the players on the tour. That's why she's doing what she's doing. Yeah, what she's doing, it's a goal for every player to be on the top for, like, so long and be consistently there. That's something unbelievable. She's serving well. She can use the slice, which is for most of the girls a really uncomfortable shot. She can hit the ball pretty heavy. She has everything in her hand, so she can do everything. That's what's makes her stronger than everybody."

Even Karolina Pliskova, denied by Ash of a first Wimbledon crown, spoke through tears to recognise the great performance that defeated her: "I think Ash played an incredible tournament and an incredible match today. Actually all the match I think she did great stuff. She was playing well. I think maybe one of the best matches she played against me because we played couple times."

And when Ash loses, as she did so surprisingly at the US Open in 2021, the woman who caused the upset was full of praise. Shelby Rogers was no doubt ecstatic about her own performance but took the trouble to laud the World No. 1: "She is one of the most professional people I've ever met in my life, as well as a good person, a funny individual," Rogers said post-match.

"She's super down to earth. I mean, she is one of my favourite people. She's resetting on the road. She's worked through some injuries on the road. She's won five titles. She's remained number one. I mean this girl is everything every player wants to be.

"Honestly, I could do this for another 20 minutes. She's one of my favourite people, so anytime I get to give her a hug, I try to take the moment."

The respect was reciprocated: "She's one that I respect, one of the most that I respect on tour, and she's an incredible person. Tonight she showed a lot of fight," Ash said.

Tennis Australia Chief Executive Officer Craig Tiley said Ash's genuine, down-to-earth charm fuelled an unprecedented boom in Australian tennis.

"There's no doubt about the Ash effect, no doubt!" he says. "Ash is a superstar — the best in the world — but she's a great person too and that's a big part of her appeal. People love watching her play because she has such a beautiful game, but we love her character too.

"Australians are right on board Ash's journey and she is creating a legacy which will last long beyond her own career."

After the 2021 US Open, Ash was announced by the US Tennis Association as the Open Women's Sportsperson for 2021. The USTA awards were instituted in 2011 to "educate and inspire youngsters and their parents to develop and exhibit a high degree of sportspersonship and an attitude of fair play and mutual respect on and off the tennis court. Underlying the charge is the ethical imperative that fairness is more important than winning."

How does Ash see herself?

"I'm just working as hard as I can to be the best I can be. It's a beautiful game and it's a privilege to play it."

There's mutual respect for the game and for the people. That's Ashleigh Barty.

*Statistics, match reports and interviews from WTA Tour and WTA Insider.*

34

# DREAMS DO COME TRUE

- Won the Wimbledon girls' singles title in 2011 at age 15, beating Irina Khromacheva in the final.
- Career goal was making the top 10 in women's tennis. Ranked 669 in 2011.
- Made her Women's Tennis Association debut at the Brisbane International in 2012.
- Secured a wildcard for her first Grand Slam event — the 2012 Australian Open.
- Won her maiden ITF Futures Pro Tour title on home soil in Sydney in 2012, followed by wins in Mildura and Nottingham.
- Stepped away from tennis in late 2014; briefly pursued a career in cricket, playing for the Brisbane Heat in the women's Big Bash League.
- Made a singles comeback in late May 2016 after a 21-month break; went 11-2 in her first two events on grass in Eastbourne (ITF) and Nottingham (WTA).
- Came via qualifying to win her first WTA title in Kuala Lumpur in March 2017.

- Cracked the top 100 on 6 March 2017, at world No. 92.
- Won her second WTA title at the Nottingham Open in June 2018.
- Won her first Grand Slam title with American CoCo Vandeweghe in the US Open doubles, September 2018.
- Won her first WTA Premier Mandatory title at the Miami Open in March 2019, a result that saw her crack the world's top 10.
- Won her first Grand Slam singles title at the French Open in June 2019.
- Reached a career-high singles ranking of No. 1 on 24 June 2019, just the second Australian woman to reach No. 1, after Evonne Goolagong Cawley in 1976. She started 2019 as No. 15.
- Received The Don award in October 2019, after being recognised as the Australian sports star who most inspired the nation that year; also topped the *Australian Financial Review*'s list of the "most culturally powerful Australians in 2019".
- Ended the 2019 season as world No. 1, the first Australian female player in WTA rankings history to top the season-ending rankings.
- Earned $US 11.3 million in 2019, the most prizemoney ever earned by an Australian player, male or female, in a single season. • Earnings included the largest prize in tennis by winning the WTA play-offs in Shenzhen, China.
- Sat out most of the 2020 season due to challenges posed by

COVID-19 lockdowns. Remained world No. 1 into 2021 and won the women's championship at her golf club, Brookwater, in Queensland.

- Won the Open Championship at Wimbledon in July 2021, defeating Karolina Pliskova 6-3, 6-7 (4-7), 6-3.

## OTHER AWARDS INCLUDE:

Australian Women's Health Sport Awards Sportswoman of the Year 2019; Moment of The Year 2019. Australian Tennis Awards Newcombe Medal 2017, 2018; Female Junior Athlete of the Year 2010, 2011, 2012,2013. National Dreamtime Awards Female Sportsperson 2017, 2018. International Tennis Federation Fed Cup Heart Award 2019. Sportsmanship award US Open 2018. People's Choice AIS Sport Performance Awards 2019 Female Athlete of the Year, ABC Sport Personality of the Year and Sporting Moment of the Year WTA Player of the Year 2019. Queensland Young Australian of the Year 2020.

Dreams achieved, but the promise of more. The one coveted title that had frustratingly eluded her: the Australian Open Championship.